LITERARY BRITAIN
AND IRELAND

A GUIDE TO THE PLACES THAT INSPIRED GREAT WRITERS

JANE STRUTHERS
CHRIS COE

NEW
HOLLAND

CONTENTS

FOREWORD

Reading a book is one of the great joys in life. It involves entering the world of an author's imagination and spending time with them while they recount their tale to us. It's no wonder that our favourite authors can start to feel like old friends, because we take so much pleasure from being in their company. We may never meet them, but we feel we know them in some essential way, because we have heard their voices, been touched by their emotions and viewed life from their perspective. This is true whether the writer in question is a poet, playwright, novelist, critic or essayist.

Every great writer creates his or her own world, often with a basis in reality, whether it is Graham Greene's 'Greeneland', Thomas Hardy's 'Wessex', Daphne du Maurier's Cornwall or William Wordsworth's Lake Ditrict, and although the writing takes us to these places in our minds it is fascinating to actually visit them. This is nothing new. When Alfred, Lord Tennyson visited Lyme Regis in Dorset the first thing he wanted to see was the Cobb where Louisa Musgrove fell down in Jane Austen's *Persuasion*.

Literary Britain and Ireland is a guide to more than 120 places associated with writers. For every entry you'll also find, where appropriate, contact details, travel information and a useful website. Wherever possible, I have chosen places that are open to the public, whether they are the houses that the authors lived in or the graveyards where they are buried. There are also museums dedicated to their memories, statues that celebrate their lives and landscapes that inspired them. The book is arranged geographically into nine regions, covering England, Scotland, Wales and both Northern Ireland and Eire, with maps to show where the places can be found so you can visit them yourself.

Of course, these places are a personal choice because it would be impossible to cram every house, church, town, village and landscape in Britain and Ireland with a literary connection into a single illustrated work. I, therefore, selected the locations that are irrevocably associated with a particular author, such as Hill Top Farm, where Beatrix Potter once lived, and those that have the strongest or most interesting links, such as Howth Head where Erskine Childers rowed ashore with a cargo of illegal guns.

The most celebrated English, Welsh, Scottish and Irish writers are included, among them Virginia Woolf, Dylan Thomas, Sir Walter Scott and W.B. Yeats. But there are also many lesser-known names, and the book covers a range of genres, including travel writing, comic novels, light fiction, pot-boilers, crime novels, gothic chillers, serious poems, humorous verse, children's novels, autobiographies, biographies, memoirs and stream of consciousness fiction.

As well as getting enjoyment from reading the book itself, and visiting the places it mentions, I hope that your interest will be awakened in those writers whose work you have never read before so the book introduces you to some new friends as well as reuniting you with old ones.

Jane Struthers

SOUTH-WEST ENGLAND

From the elegant Regency crescents of Bath to the rugged coastline of Cornwall, from the wilds of Dartmoor to the palm trees of Torquay, the south-west of England offers a rich variety of moods and landscapes. It has inspired many great writers, some of whom have created their own worlds within these counties. Thomas Hardy, while living and writing in his native Dorset, conjured up the mythical county of Wessex in which many of his novels were set. Daphne du Maurier's imagination and heart were similarly captured by Cornwall, prompting her to write a succession of period romances and novels that were inspired by the countryside and houses around Fowey. The magic of the West Country continues to captivate contemporary writers, including John Fowles who wrote about Lyme Regis, where he lived, and Sean O'Casey, who spent many years living in Devon.

Legend:

1. Padstow
2. St Enodoc
3. Godrevy Lighthouse
4. Higher Tregerthen
5. Fowey
6. Torquay
7. Sidmouth
8. Lyme Regis
9. Clouds Hill
10. Thomas Hardy's Cottage
11. Salisbury
12. Bath
13. Coleridge Cottage

○ City
○ Town or village

N

PADSTOW

CORNWALL

See map p.9 (1)

KEY FIGURES: Sir John Betjeman; Sir Walter Raleigh
KEY LOCATIONS: Daymer Bay; Wadebridge; South Quay

Northern Cornwall has been attracting visitors for centuries. It was the spiritual home of the celebrated poet Sir John Betjeman (1906–84). As far as he was concerned, there was 'splendour, splendour everywhere' throughout the county, which he had loved since he first visited Daymer Bay as a boy.

Betjeman chronicled his love of Cornwall in both poetry and prose, including such disparate works as *The Shell Guide to Cornwall* (1934) and *Summoned by Bells* (1960). The latter, an autobiography in blank-verse that spans the period from his childhood until he went to university at Oxford, described Betjeman's enjoyment of his Cornish sojourns.

Betjeman described his personal experience of Cornwall, of coming home on the Padstow ferry 'on a fine, still evening, laden with the week's shopping', and his particular fondness of the stretch of railway that spans from Wadebridge to Padstow.

Betjeman's book, *Cornwall* (1964), is an idiosyncratic guide to the places that he knew, taking the reader across beaches, into coves and around tiny churches. His love of the county is commemorated in the Betjeman Centre, which is situated at the railway station in Wadebridge and contains fascinating information about Betjeman's connections with the area.

Betjeman was not the first poet to have discovered the delights of Padstow and its surrounding countryside, however. The Elizabethan courtier and poet Sir Walter Raleigh (*c.*1554–1618) was Warden of Cornwall from 1585 and stayed at Raleigh's Court House on South Quay in Padstow when he was in the county. Although still standing, Raleigh's house is not open to the public, sadly.

(i) information

Contact details

Padstow
Cornwall

☎ Tourist Information:
+44 (0)1841 533 449

www Tourist Information:
www.padstowlive.com

Betjeman Centre:
www.johnbetjeman.org.uk

Transport links

🚆 Bodmin Parkway

🚗 The A389 passes through Padstow, as does the B3276

ST ENODOC
CORNWALL

See map p.9 (2)

KEY FIGURES: Sir John Betjeman; Thomas Hardy
KEY LOCATIONS: Rock; St Juliot's Church

As Poet Laureate, Sir John Betjeman could have opted for burial in London's Westminster Abbey when he died from Parkinson's Disease in 1984, but he elected to be buried in the churchyard at St Enodoc in Rock. Betjeman had a particular love of old churches and took great pleasure in exploring those in his beloved Cornwall.

St Juliot, a 13th-century church, lies a few miles to the north-east of St Enodoc. In 1870, the Reverend Gifford, the rector, asked a young architect named Thomas Hardy (1840–1928) to give his opinion on the restoration of the church. When Hardy called at the rectory, he met and fell in love with the rector's sister-in-law, Emma. The

▲ *Sir John Betjeman, pictured above reading poetry, loved Northern Cornwall.*

couple were subsequently married in 1874. In memory of this, Hardy recreated St Juliot as St Agnes in his 1873 novel *A Pair of Blue Eyes*.

(i) information

Contact details

St Enodoc
Rock
Cornwall

 Cornwall Guide (Rock):
www.cornwalls.co.uk/Rock

Transport links

🚆 Roche

🚌 The B3314 passes near St Enodoc

GODREVY LIGHTHOUSE
CORNWALL

See map p.9　③

KEY FIGURE:	Virginia Woolf; Rupert Brooke
KEY LOCATIONS:	Talland House; St Ives

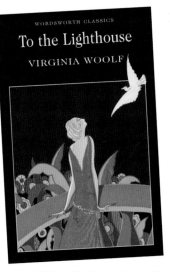

Each summer the Stephen family spent their holidays at Talland House, near St Ives. Sir Leslie Stephen (1832–1904) bought the house in 1882, the same year that his youngest child, Virginia (1882–1941), was born. The house was always full of visitors, including a young Rupert Brooke (1887–1915), who went on to become a celebrated poet. The Stephen family, including Virginia's siblings – Vanessa, Thoby and Adrian – continued to visit St Ives until just before the death of Virginia's mother, Julia, in 1895. The Stephen children revisited St Ives and Talland House in the summer of 1905, after the death of their father the year before.

For the most part the happy memories of her time in St Ives and Talland House emerged in several novels Virginia wrote under her married name 'Woolf', including *Jacob's Room* (1922), *The Waves* (1931) and, most notably, *To the Lighthouse* (1927; shown left). *To the Lighthouse* drew on her memories of the Cornish countryside around Godrevy Lighthouse, which stands close to the bay of St Ives and is visible for miles around. Although she set the book in the Hebrides, it is full of her feelings towards Cornwall. The first part of the novel also features the gracious Mrs Ramsey and emotionally demanding Mr Ramsey, who are based on Virginia's parents.

ⓘ information

Contact details

Godrevy Lighthouse
Gwithian (near Hayle)
Cornwall, TR27 5ED

+44 (0)1208 265212

National Trust:
www.nationaltrust.org.uk/main/
w-godrevy

Transport links

Hayle

The A30 passes near Gwithian and the B3301 passes through

HIGHER TREGERTHEN
CORNWALL

See map p.9 (4)

KEY FIGURES: D.H. Lawrence; Katherine Mansfield; John Middleton Murry
KEY LOCATIONS: The Tinker's Arms; Zennor

In March 1916, D.H. Lawrence (1885–1930) and his wife, Frieda, moved from London to Cornwall. Lawrence's health was ailing and they dreamed of creating a small literary community with New Zealand-born novelist Katherine Mansfield (1888–1923), and her lover and later husband, John Middleton Murry (1889–1957).

The Lawrences found two adjoining cottages available in Higher Tregerthen, a short distance from Zennor. Mansfield and Murry arrived in April but the literary commune soon disbanded. Lawrence reflected on that time in the novel *Women in Love* (1920), which casts himself and Frieda as Birkin and Ursula, and Katherine and Murry as Gudrun and Gerald. The Murrys were not pleased when they read it. Literary hostess Lady Ottoline Morrell (1873–1938) also ended her friendship with Lawrence after recognizing herself in the eccentric character of Hermione.

▲ *D.H. Lawrence and his wife stayed at the Tinker's Arms in Zennor while searching for cottages to rent.*

The Lawrences left Higher Tregerthen in October 1917. Following the growing suspicion that they were German spies, the cottage was raided by the police and some of Lawrence's manuscripts were taken away for examination. The couple returned to London where they lived for two years before moving to Italy.

ⓘ information

Contact details

Tregerthen
St Ives
Cornwall, TR26 1HA

🖳 Cornwall Guide (Zennor):
www.cornwalls.co.uk/Zennor

Transport links

🚆 St Ives

🚗 The A3074 passes through St Ives

FOWEY
CORNWALL

See map p.9 (5)

KEY FIGURES: Kenneth Grahame; Sir Arthur Quiller-Couch; Daphne du Maurier
KEY LOCATIONS: St Fimbarrus' Church; The Haven; Ferryside; Menabilly

KENNETH GRAHAME
The Wind in the Willows

Fowey has long drawn many writers and artists to its beautiful shores.

Kenneth Grahame (1859–1932), author of the children's classic *The Wind in the Willows* (1908; shown left) first visited Fowey in 1899 and was entranced by the place. He married Elspeth Thomson in July of that year at St Fimbarrus' Church with his great friend, Sir Arthur Quiller-Couch (1863–1944) in attendance. After a short honeymoon, Grahame and his wife returned to Fowey where he and Quiller-Couch spent most of their time boating around the lovely coast.

Quiller-Couch, popularly known as 'Q', lived and worked in The Haven, on the Esplanade in Fowey, from 1892 until his death in 1944. Q was a prolific writer whose first adventure story, *Dead Man's Rock*, was published in 1887. A year later he wrote *The Astonishing History of Troy Town*, based on Fowey, the first of several novels about the town, whose mayor he became in 1937.

In 1907, the Grahames returned to Cornwall for a short holiday while their only child, Alastair, stayed in Sussex with his governess. Grahame's letters to his son formed the beginnings of what was to become *The Wind in the Willows*. Grahame and his family later settled in Fowey after his retirement in 1907.

Fowey is also immortalized in the novels of Daphne du Maurier (1907–89). In 1926 the du Maurier family bought Ferryside, a holiday home situated next to the Bodinnick ferry. The young Daphne often stayed on in Cornwall after her family had returned to London each year, and busied herself exploring the coastline both on foot and by boat. She also spent the time writing intensely, and her first novel, *The Loving Spirit*, was published to huge acclaim in 1931. By this time she was great friends with the Quiller-Couch family and often went riding with their daughter, Foy, over Bodmin Moor.

The Loving Spirit made such an impact on a certain Major Tommy 'Boy' Browning that he sailed into Fowey harbour to meet its author.

▲ *Daphne du Maurier wrote her first novel,* The Loving Spirit *(1931), while staying in her family's holiday home, Ferryside, in Fowey.*

The result of this meeting could have come straight from one of Daphne's novels – they fell in love and were married in July 1932 at St Wyllow's Church, Lanteglos.

Daphne had fallen deeply in love once before when, in 1927, she stumbled across the house that obsessed her for the rest of her life. This was Menabilly, which she turned into Manderley in her celebrated gothic thriller-romance, *Rebecca* (1938). She finally managed to live there in 1943, but only as a tenant because the owners –

the Rashleigh family – refused to sell it to her. The house was also the setting for *The King's General* (1946) and *My Cousin Rachel* (1951).

The inevitable happened in 1967, when the lease on Menabilly ran out and Daphne was forced to leave. She moved to Kilmarth, above Polkerris, which she used as the setting for *The House on the Strand* (1969), but she still yearned for Menabilly. She wrote about her love for her adoptive county in almost all her books, and died in Par in April 1989.

ⓘ information

Contact details

Fowey
Cornwall

☎ Tourist Information:
+44 (0)1726 833616

www Tourist Information:
www.fowey.co.uk

Daphne du Maurier Festival:
www.dumaurierfestival.co.uk

Transport links

🚆 St Austell and Par

🚗 The A3082 and the B3269 pass through Fowey

TORQUAY
DEVON

See map p.9　6

KEY FIGURES:　　Elizabeth Barrett; Agatha Christie; Sean O'Casey
KEY LOCATIONS:　Hotel Regina; Babbacombe Bay; Torre Abbey

In August 1838, the poet Elizabeth Barrett (1806–61) was sent to the Devon resort of Torquay for the sake of her health. Elizabeth was fully accustomed to the life of an invalid, but was outraged when her Torquay doctor forbade her to write, despite the fact that she had already published a volume of verse, *The Seraphim, and Other Poems*, to critical acclaim in June of that year. With her brother Edward, whom she called 'Bro', Elizabeth settled at 1 Beacon Terrace (where the Hotel Regina now stands).

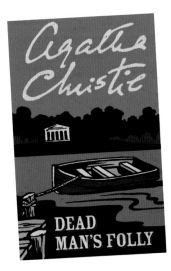

In February 1840, the siblings received the news that their brother, Sam, had died of fever in Jamaica – but worse was to come.

In July, Bro went sailing but didn't return. Elizabeth was distraught when

▲ *Hercule Poirot travels on what is today the Paignton and Dartmouth Steam Train in* Dead Man's Folly.

his body was washed up in Babbacombe Bay. Elizabeth was finally allowed to return to London in September 1841. Her stay in Torquay was one of the worst experiences of her life.

The writer who is perhaps most associated with Torquay, however, is crime-fiction writer Agatha Christie (1890–1976), who wrote over 70 detective novels set in a respectable, upper-middle-class world of teashops, maids, ruthless spinsters and ageing colonels. Born Agatha Miller, she was baptized at All Saints Church, Bampfylde Road, when she was two months old. Partly through the generosity of Agatha's father, the church had been rebuilt and Agatha was listed as a founder member of the church, despite being an infant at the time.

As a teenager, Agatha worked on Saturdays in a pharmacy in Trematon Avenue, where she learned a great deal about poisons – poisoning is a method particularly favoured by her characters. She later trained as a pharmacist and worked in the dispensary at Torre Hospital during both world wars.

Like all writers, Agatha drew heavily on her own life and experiences in her books, and many places in Torquay were reproduced in

▲ *Agatha Christie typed many of her books on this 1937 Remington typewriter, which is part of an exhibition dedicated to the detective fiction writer at Torre Abbey in Torquay.*

her novels. She regularly took the steam train from Paignton to Churston, and her Belgian detective Hercule Poirot travelled on this line in *The ABC Murders* (1936) and *Dead Man's Folly* (1956). Agatha, in turn, is remembered in many different sites throughout Torquay, and a special room is devoted to her memory at Torre Abbey. She lived in Torquay until 1938, but later owned Greenway, in Galmpton near Brixham, which is now open to the public through the National

Trust. Visitors to Torquay can take in 10 sites associated with the writer – including the Imperial Hotel and Beacon Cove, where Agatha bathed as a girl – in what is known as the Agatha Christie Mile.

The Irish playwright, Sean O'Casey (1880–1964) is also associated with the town. He moved with his wife, Eileen, to the suburb of St Marychurch in Torquay in 1954 and lived here until his death 10 years later.

ⓘ information

Contact details
Torquay
Devon

 Local Information:
www.torquay.com

Transport links
🚆 Torquay

🚌 The A3022 passes through Torquay

SIDMOUTH
DEVON

See map p.9 (7)

KEY FIGURE: Elizabeth Barrett
KEY LOCATIONS: 7–8 Fortfield Terrace; All Saints Road

The precarious health of the young poet, Miss Elizabeth Barrett, was a torment to her widowed father, Edward, for years. She suffered from a weak chest, which may have been caused by tuberculosis, and she also showed signs of what is now understood to be anorexia nervosa. Another torment to Edward was his financial state, which led to the sale of the family house in Hope End, Ledbury, Hertfordshire, in August 1832 when Elizabeth was 26. The family decamped to Sidmouth in Devon, an elegant seaside town that was considered beneficial for Elizabeth's health. At first they stayed at 7–8 Fortfield Terrace, moving to Belle Vue (now the Cedar Shade Hotel) in All Saints Road the following year.

Although most of the large Barrett family enjoyed life at the seaside, Elizabeth felt starved of intellectual company. She compensated for

▲ *Elizabeth Barrett came to Sidmouth in 1832, in the hope that the balmy air would improve her health.*

this by working on a translation from the Greek of *Prometheus Bound* by Aeschylus, as well as 19 poems, which were published in May 1833. In the autumn of 1835 the family moved to Wimpole Street, London, a move that also saw the return of Elizabeth's ill-health.

(i) information

Contact details

Sidmouth
Devon

[www] Local Information:
www.visitsidmouth.co.uk

☎ +44 (0)1395 512424

Transport links

🚆 Exeter St David's
Honiton

🚗 The A3052 passes
near Sidmouth

LYME REGIS
DORSET

See map p.9   (8)

KEY FIGURES: Jane Austen; John Fowles
KEY LOCATIONS: The Assembly Rooms; The Cobb

In the summer of 1804, the Austen family stayed at the seaside town of Lyme Regis, which had become fashionable. Among the party was Jane (1775–1817), who was trying hard to become a published writer. Jane was a prolific letter writer, particularly to her sister, Cassandra (1773–1845), who left Lyme Regis that September to stay with their brother, Henry, and his wife, Eliza, in Weymouth. In a letter to Cassandra, Jane described her experiences in Lyme Regis, including dancing in the Assembly Rooms and wearing herself out by bathing in the sea. She also walked along the Cobb, the stone jetty that projects out to sea from the shore.

Jane used her experiences as inspiration for an important scene in *Persuasion* (1817). Louisa Musgrove has to be 'jumped down' the steps of the Cobb by Captain Wentworth, but falls and is 'taken up lifeless'. When Alfred, Lord Tennyson

▲ *The stone jetty, or the Cobb, is the setting for Louisa Musgrove's fall in* Persuasion.

(1809–92) visited Lyme Regis, he cried, 'Show me the steps from which Louisa Musgrove fell!'

The Cobb was immortalized again in print by John Fowles in *The French Lieutenant's Woman* (1969). His mysterious heroine has a habit of standing on the Cobb staring out to sea.

(i) information

Contact details
Lyme Regis
Dorset

Local Information:
www.lymeregis.org

☎ +44 (0)1297 442138

Transport links
Axminster

The A3052 passes through Lyme Regis

CLOUDS HILL
DORSET

See map p.9   (9)

KEY FIGURES: T.E. Lawrence; Eric Kennington
KEY LOCATIONS: Clouds Hill; Moreton; Wareham

T.E. Lawrence (1888–1935) first rented Clouds Hill in 1923. He loved the house, saying that it reminded him of Egdon Heath in Thomas Hardy's novel *The Return of the Native* (1878).

In 1924, Lawrence wrote to a friend that he came to Clouds Hill '… nearly every evening, and dream, or write or read by the fire.' He was revising the manuscript of *The Seven Pillars of Wisdom* (1935), his account of the Arab Revolt, for which he received great encouragement from friends E.M. Forster, Thomas Hardy and George Bernard Shaw.

By the time that Lawrence was discharged from the RAF in February 1935, he had purchased Clouds Hill. One of his greatest pleasures in life was riding motorcycles and he loved roaring along the Dorset lanes on whichever 'wild beast' he happened to own at the time. He was killed in May 1935,

▲ *T. E. Lawrence wrote his best-known work,* The Seven Pillars of Wisdom, *while living at Clouds Hill.*

after being thrown headfirst into the road. He is buried in the churchyard of St Nicholas's Church, Moreton. There is also a memorial to him at St Martin's Church, Wareham: it is a stone effigy of him in Arab costume, which was sculpted by his friend, Eric Kennington (1888–1960).

(i) information

Contact details

Clouds Hill
Wareham
Dorset, BH20 7NQ

National Trust (Clouds Hill):
www.nationaltrust.org.uk

Tourist Information:
☎ +44 (0)1929 405616

Transport links

🚃 Wool, Moreton

🚗 The A351 passes by Wareham

THOMAS HARDY'S DORSET
DORSET

See map p.9 (10)

KEY FIGURES:	Thomas Hardy; Cecil Day-Lewis
KEY LOCATIONS:	Hardy's Birthplace; Max Gate; Stinsford Church

Dorset provided the inspiration for some of Thomas Hardy's most revered books. Hardy knew Dorset all of his life. He grew up in the cottage now called Hardy's Birthplace in Higher Bockhampton, but left for London in 1874 with his first wife, Emma. For a time the Hardys oscillated between London and Dorset, but they finally moved to Max Gate in their home county in 1885. Today, both cottages are open to the public.

Hardy's Cottage

This tiny rural dwelling is where Hardy was born and spent the first 24 years of his life. Even today the cottage can only be reached by a 10-minute walk through the woods, and when the young Hardy was growing up here he had to tramp 6 miles to his school in Dorchester each morning, and then do the return journey in the evening. This exposure to the outdoors encouraged an acute awareness of his surroundings, and his novels are notable for their detailed descriptions of the Dorset countryside.

In his second published novel, *Under the Greenwood Tree* (1872), Hardy's Cottage appears as Tranter Dewy's house, and Hardy wrote the

▲ *Thomas Hardy loved Dorset. It featured heavily in his writing.*

book in his bedroom there. *Far from the Madding Crowd* (1874) was also written at the cottage, and when the weather was fine Hardy wrote in the garden. However, there were drawbacks to this, as he sometimes ran out of paper at the point where inspiration was beginning to flow, and, rather than risk breaking his train of thought by going indoors, he wrote on whatever came to hand, whether it was an old leaf or a piece of slate.

▲ Hardy entertained his fellow writers in his drawing room at Max Gate.

Max Gate

By the time *Far from the Madding Crowd* was published, Hardy had moved out of the cottage and was living in less rural surroundings in Surbiton, Surrey, with his wife, Emma. He wanted to return to Dorset not only for health reasons, but because he wanted to stay close to his family. Besides, his writing was so steeped in Dorset and its neighbouring counties — which he called Wessex in his novels — that he needed to live in the region to gain inspiration from it.

Hardy was trained as an architect, so he naturally wanted to design his new home in Dorchester. Under his supervision, Hardy's brother and father began building the house in November 1883, and the Hardys spent their first night in the small cottage in June 1885. Some years later when Hardy felt more financially secure, he decided to build extensions onto the cottage, which almost doubled it in size. Although Hardy described Max Gate as 'only a cottage in the country which I use for writing in', it was much more imposing than that and proclaimed loudly that Hardy had graduated from his humble beginnings to an enviable prosperity. Nevertheless, Hardy spent a substantial part of each year in London or abroad, and Max Gate sometimes felt 'lonely and cottage-like' to him. It did not help that the Hardys' marriage was largely unhappy and emotionally chilly, although Hardy looked back on it with romantic nostalgia in the love poems he wrote after Emma's sudden death in 1912.

Hardy wrote his later novels while cloistered in his study at Max Gate – *The Mayor of Casterbridge* (1886), *The Woodlanders* (1887), *Tess of the D'Urbervilles* (1891; shown right), *The Well-Beloved* (1892) and his final novel, *Jude the Obscure* (1895). Hardy had long chafed under the criticisms of reviewers who complained of the immoral and pessimistic nature of his novels, but the controversy over the publication of *Jude the Obscure*, which involved adult seduction and child suicide, was so great that he felt compelled to stop writing novels altogether. He concentrated on his poetry instead, which, despite never receiving the same recognition as his novels, Hardy had always loved.

After Emma's death – some of his verse suggested that her ghost haunted Max Gate – Hardy married Florence Dugdale in 1914. Although immersed in his poetry, he also

had a busy social life, entertaining the literary lions of the day, including the poet Siegfried Sassoon (1886–1967), T.E. Lawrence – who lived nearby at Clouds Hill (see page 20), J.M. Barrie (1860–1937), W.B. Yeats (1865–1939) and Virginia Woolf.

Hardy died at Max Gate in January 1928. Just as in life he had divided his time between Dorset and London, so in death he did the same: his heart was buried near the family graves in Stinsford church and his ashes were interred in Westminster Abbey (see page 72). This arrangement went against Hardy's personal wish to be buried in Stinsford, but he was such a literary giant by the time of his death that it was generally felt that the abbey was the most fitting place for him. The Poet Laureate Cecil Day-Lewis (1904–72), who was a tremendous fan of Hardy, was also buried in Stinsford churchyard in 1972.

ⓘ information

Contact details

Thomas Hardy's Birthplace
Higher Bockhampton
Dorchester
Dorset
DT2 8QJ

Max Gate
Winfrith Newburgh
Dorchester
Dorset
DT2 8JR

☎ +44 (0)1305 262366   ☎ +44 (0)1297 489481

Transport links

🚆 Dorchester South
Dorchester West

🚗 The A35 passes through Dorchester

SALISBURY

WILTSHIRE

KEY FIGURES: Samuel Pepys; Anthony Trollope; Thomas Hardy; Charles Dickens; E.M. Forster; William Golding; George Herbert

KEY LOCATIONS: Old George Mall; Salisbury Cathedral; Figsbury Rings; Cathedral Close

The city of Salisbury has many literary associations and writers as wide ranging as Charles Dickens and William Golding have been inspired to write about it.

On 10 June 1668, Samuel Pepys recorded in his diary that he thought the city of Salisbury was 'greater than Oxford'. However, he was less impressed with the quality of his lodgings, which were at the George Inn. This 14th-century coaching inn has now vanished except for its gables, which can still be seen above the entrance to the Old George Mall. Pepys also visited Stonehenge, which he found most impressive despite being puzzled about why it had ever been built.

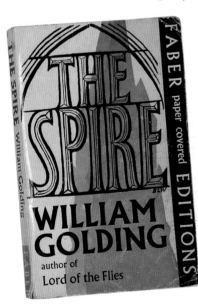

▲ *The Spire was based on William Golding's own experiences of living in Salisbury.*

An evening stroll around Salisbury Cathedral provided the idea for writer Anthony Trollope (1815–82), who set his novel *The Warden* (1855) in the cathedral town of Barchester. His fictional town also borrowed heavily on nearby Winchester (see pages 32–3).

For Thomas Hardy, many years later, Salisbury became Melchester in his sequence of Wessex novels. It features particularly in *Jude the Obscure* (1895), and is where Jude's cousin and great love, Sue Bridehead, goes to college. The relationship ends in tragedy, and the novel was considered to be so depressing and immoral that Hardy never wrote another work of fiction.

Charles Dickens also made great use of Salisbury in his favourite novel *Martin Chuzzlewit* (1844), as the home of the egregious widower and hypocrite, Mr Pecksniff. When Tom Pinch, who is Mr Pecksniff's assistant, arrives in Salisbury he 'set forth on a stroll about the streets with a vague and not unpleasant idea that they teemed with all kinds of mystery and bedevilment'. However, most of the bedevilment in his life came from his employer.

Novelist E.M. Forster (1879–1970) was also very fond of Salisbury Cathedral, believing it had 'the most beautiful spire in the world'. Forster was familiar with the city because he used to stay with friends at 13 New Canal. Aged 25, he visited Figsbury Rings outside Salisbury where he met a shepherd boy, who inspired his love of the landscape. Forster wrote about the Figsbury Rings as the Cadbury Rings in *The Longest Journey* (1907).

From 1945 to 1962 William Golding (1911–93) taught English at Bishop Wordsworth's School in the Cathedral Close. It was during this period of his life that he wrote *Lord of the Flies* (1954), his classic novel about a group of schoolboys trapped on a desert island whose society descends into inhumanity. It was his first novel and an instant success. Later, Golding wrote *The Spire* (1964), which centred on one man's determination to build a massively tall spire for a cathedral despite what anyone else might think of his plans.

The steeple of Salisbury Cathedral was the inspiration for William Golding's The Spire. ▶

Inside Salisbury Cathedral is a memorial window to the poet George Herbert (1593–1633), who was ordained in the cathedral and then became rector of St Andrew's in the nearby parish of Bemerton. He wrote much of his poetry in the rectory, and used to walk over the fields to the cathedral.

Herbert died of consumption in 1633 and was buried in the chancel of his church. The stained glass window in his memory was installed in 1953. A statue of the poet was erected outside Salisbury Cathedral as part of its millennium project.

ⓘ information

Contact details

Salisbury
Wiltshire

☎ +44 (0)8456 027323

🖳 Local Information:
www.visitwiltshire.co.uk/salisbury

Transport links

🚋 Salisbury

🚗 The A30 passes by Salisbury

BATH
SOMERSET

See map p.9 (12)

KEY FIGURES: Dr Samuel Johnson; Fanny Burney; Richard Brinsley Sheridan; Thomas De Quincey; Jane Austen; Charles Dickens; Walter Savage Landor

KEY LOCATIONS: Royal Crescent; Green Park Buldings; St James Square; New King Street

From the 17th century onwards, Bath was one of the most fashionable cities in the whole of Britain.It was an important place to be seen, and writers were just as susceptible to the need to be in the vanguard of the latest trend as anyone else. In 1668 the diarist Samuel Pepys (1633–1703) travelled to Bath to take the famous waters, although he was rather dubious about the hygiene of so many naked bodies crowding into one small bathing pool.

Dr Samuel Johnson (1709–84), the author of the first dictionary in the English language, visited Bath in 1776, accompanied by his great travelling companions, Hester Thrale (1740–1821) and her husband Henry

(*c.*1730–1781). The Thrales returned four years later to stay at 14 South Parade, and this time they brought their friend Fanny Burney (1752–1840), who used her experiences as inspiration for her writing. Her first novel, *Evelina*, was published anonymously in 1778.

When Fanny came to Bath she had just been revealed as the author of *Evelina* and was basking in her new-found celebrity. Three years after the death of Henry Thrale in 1781, Hester married an Italian musician named Gabriel Piozzi in Bath, much to the consternation of her friends, including Dr Johnson and Fanny Burney.

In 1772, Bath's Royal Crescent was the scene of a romantic adventure that inspired Richard

Brinsley Sheridan (1751–1816) to write his great comic play *The Rivals*. While living with his parents in New King Street, the young Sheridan fell in love with a singer, Eliza Linley, who lived at 11 Royal Crescent. She was very beautiful, and Sheridan found he had a rival for her affections in one Captain Matthews. To remove her from the path of his opponent, Sheridan carried Eliza off to France. However, Matthews was still smitten by Eliza when she returned to England with Sheridan, who felt duty-bound to fight two duels with Matthews before taking his beloved to London and marrying her. *The Rivals*, which was first performed in 1775, is set in Bath, with Captain Absolute in Sheridan's role and Lydia Languish in that of Eliza's.

The young Thomas De Quincey (1785–1859), the author of *Confessions of an English Opium Eater* (1822), attended Bath Grammar School from 1796 to 1799, while living at 6 Green Park Buildings.

One of the most famous literary associations with Bath is that of Jane Austen. In 1804, following her father's retirement, Jane lived

▲ *Richard Sheridan set his play* The Rivals *in the Royal Crescent (shown below).*

with her parents at 27 Green Park Buildings, during which time she worked on her novel *The Watsons*, which she abandoned after her father's death in 1805. The Austens had previously lived at 1 The Paragon and then 4 Sidney Place. Although Jane had enjoyed spending holidays

JANE AUSTEN'S BATH

Think of Bath and most people call to mind the town of Jane Austen's Regency novels – the Pump Room, the Assembly Rooms and the Royal Crescent. In fact, Austen only set two of her novels in Bath, the Gothic Northanger Abbey and Persuasion (both 1818), her last novel. Both recreate the streets and architecture of the time. Northanger Abbey describes the Royal Crescent as a place where people go to 'breathe the fresh air of better people' and heroine Catherine Morland visits the Pump Rooms to watch Bath society. In Persuasion, protagonist Anne Elliot moves to Bath to be with her father, Sir Walter Elliot, and Gay Street is where Admiral and Mrs Croft live when they come to town. Today, the Jane Austen Centre is housed at 40 Gay Street. Austen once lived in this street. The Centre details the author's life and times and contains vital information about Jane Austen and her work. Each summer Bath hosts a Jane Austen festival, where visitors can experience Jane Austen's world.

entertaining pen satirized the city's society in *Persuasion* and *Northanger Abbey*, both of which were published in 1818, a year after her death (see box, left).

In 1840, the writer Charles Dickens (1812–70) visited his friend, the poet and essayist Walter Savage Landor (1775–1864), who lived at 35 St James Square. It was here that Dickens wrote Little Nell's death scene for *The Old Curiosity Shop* (1841): an event that stunned the story's many avid readers on both sides of the Atlantic. In *Bleak House* (1853) Dickens based the character of Lawrence Boythorne, who had such a passion for litigation, on Landor.

According to legend, Bath also figured prominently in another Dickens novel: the proprietor of the London–Bath coach and owner of the now-demolished White Hart Hotel in Stall Street was one Moses Pickwick, who gave his name to Samuel Pickwick in *The Posthumous Papers of the Pickwick Club* (1837). In the novel, Mr Pickwick and his fellow members of the Pickwick Club stay at Bath, first at the White Hart Hotel and then in Royal Crescent.

in Bath, she was less taken with it when she had to live here, and her mischievous but highly

ⓘ information

Contact details

Bath
Somerset

☎ +44 (0)844 8475257 (Overseas);
0906 711 2000 (UK)

🌐 Tourist Information:
www.visitbath.co.uk

Transport links

🚆 Bath

🚗 The A4 and the A36 both pass through Bath

COLERIDGE COTTAGE

SOMERSET

See map p.9 (13)

KEY FIGURES: Samuel Taylor Coleridge; William Wordsworth

KEY LOCATIONS: Nether Stowey; Alfoxden

In 1796, the Romantic poet Samuel Taylor Coleridge (1772–1834) was struggling to support his wife, Sara, their first son, Hartley, and what was becoming an increasing dependence on opium. His friend, Tom Poole, suggested that the Coleridges should come to live next door to him in Lime Street, Nether Stowey, in Somerset. Coleridge needed no prompting – especially as Poole offered him £40 to live on.

The following June, Coleridge met another man who was to have a major impact on his life – William Wordsworth (1770–1850), who moved to nearby Alfoxden with his sister, Dorothy.

▲ 'The Rime of the Ancient Mariner' etching by Gustav Doré.

The two poets collaborated on *Lyrical Ballads* (1798), a selection of their work.

Wordsworth encouraged Coleridge in his poetry. He subsequently wrote some of his greatest poetry while living at Nether Stowey, including 'The Rime of the Ancient Mariner', 'Frost at Midnight' and 'Kubla Khan'.

When the Wordsworths left Alfoxden in 1800, Coleridge missed them so much that he and his family followed them to Grasmere in the Lake District. His time at Nether Stowey was one of the happiest periods in his life and it was the place where he found it easiest to write poetry.

(i) information

Contact details

Coleridge Cottage
35 Lime Street, Nether Stowey
Bridgwater, Somerset
TA5 1NQ

☎ +44 (0)1278 732662

www National Trust (Coleridge Cottage):
www.nationaltrust.org.uk

Transport links

🚆 Bridgwater

🚗 The A39 passes through Nether Stowey

SOUTH-EAST ENGLAND

Perhaps because of its proximity to London, the south-east of England has a great many literary connections. The gentle undulations of the South Downs have attracted writers for centuries, from John Evelyn, who grew up in Lewes, to Alfred, Lord Tennyson who loved to walk through the Surrey lanes. Sussex became the home-from-home of the Bloomsbury Group, centred round Virginia and Leonard Woolf's house in Rodmell, while Hampshire has strong links with Jane Austen. Kent is forever connected with Charles Dickens, who loved the county and put many Kentish characters and places into his novels. And the holiday resort town of Brighton has drawn writers from Dr Samuel Johnson to Graham Greene, while George Orwell, Cyril Connolly and Rumer Godden all went to school in Eastbourne.

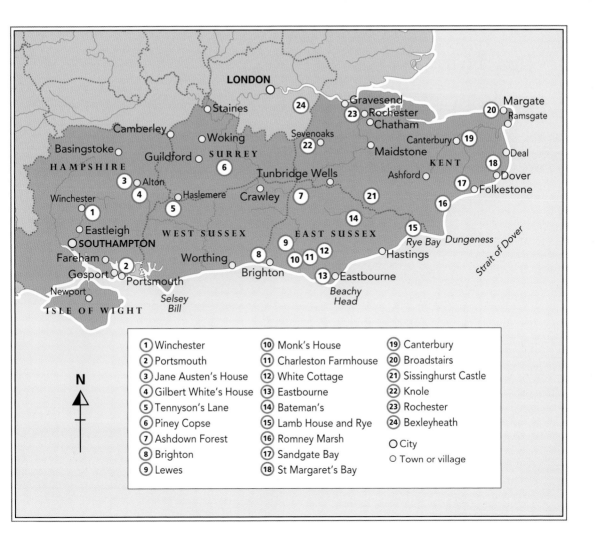

LONDON

Staines

24

Gravesend

23 Rochester

Chatham

Margate

20 Ramsgate

Camberley

Woking

Sevenoaks

Canterbury

19

Deal

Basingstoke

Guildford

SURREY

22

Maidstone

KENT

Winchester

HAMPSHIRE

3 Alton

4

6

Tunbridge Wells

Crawley

7

Ashford

18

17 Dover

Folkestone

Haslemere

5

21

16

1

Eastleigh

WEST SUSSEX

EAST SUSSEX

14

15

Rye Bay

Dungeness

Strait of Dover

SOUTHAMPTON

9

Hastings

Fareham

Worthing

8

10 11 12

Gosport

2

Brighton

13 Eastbourne

Newport

Portsmouth

Selsey

Bill

Beachy

Head

ISLE OF WIGHT

N

1 Winchester
2 Portsmouth
3 Jane Austen's House
4 Gilbert White's House
5 Tennyson's Lane
6 Piney Copse
7 Ashdown Forest
8 Brighton
9 Lewes

10 Monk's House
11 Charleston Farmhouse
12 White Cottage
13 Eastbourne
14 Bateman's
15 Lamb House and Rye
16 Romney Marsh
17 Sandgate Bay
18 St Margaret's Bay

19 Canterbury
20 Broadstairs
21 Sissinghurst Castle
22 Knole
23 Rochester
24 Bexleyheath

O City
O Town or village

WINCHESTER
HAMPSHIRE

See map p.31 (1)

KEY FIGURES: Jane Austen; Izaak Walton; Gilbert White; Sir Walter Raleigh; John Keats; Anthony Trollope; Matthew Arnold

KEY LOCATIONS: College Street; Winchester Cathedral Library

Many literary figures gained inspiration while living or working in the majestic city of Winchester, among them Jane Austen and Anthony Trollope.

When Jane Austen died in her lodgings at 8 College Street in Winchester in July 1817, she was such a celebrated writer that she was given the posthumous honour of being buried in Winchester Cathedral. Her grave is in the north aisle of the nave, and is marked with a stone tablet and a memorial window.

Jane was following in illustrious footsteps, as Izaak Walton (1593–1683) was buried in the south transept of the cathedral, in Prior Silkstede's Chapel. Although Walton wrote biographies of several important figures, including the poets John Donne (1572–1631) and George Herbert, it is *The Compleat Angler* that has gained literary immortality. It was first published in 1653 and then greatly revised for the second edition two years later.

Winchester's Cathedral Library (shown opposite) is maintained in the oldest book room in Europe. It was added to the cathedral in the 12th century. The library contains a first

▲ *Jane Austen moved to Winchester in 1817 to be closer to her physician.*

▲ *Winchester Cathedral Library has an impressive range of books, including the 1618 speech that Sir Walter Raleigh made from the scaffold.*

edition of Gilbert White's *The Natural History and Antiquities of Selborne*, which was published in 1789, as well as a copy of the speech that Sir Walter Raleigh made from the scaffold in 1618.

When poet John Keats (1795–1821) visited Winchester in the summer and early autumn of 1819 to stay with his friend Charles Armitage Brown, he commented that 'the side streets here are excessively maiden-lady-like'. The city was also familiar to Anthony Trollope,

who attended Winchester College for a short time before going to Harrow in 1827. He later based the first of his Barsetshire novels, *The Warden* (1855), which deals with the life of the warden of Hiram's Hospital, on a scandal that surrounded the master of Winchester's Hospital of St Cross in 1808.

In 1837, Matthew Arnold (1822–88) also attended Winchester College before being sent to Rugby, where his father was headmaster.

ⓘ information

Contact details

Winchester
Hampshire

☎ Tourist Information:
+44 (0)1962 840 500

🖳 Local Information:
www.visitwinchester.co.uk

Transport links

🚆 Winchester

🚗 The M3 and the A34 pass through Winchester

PORTSMOUTH

HAMPSHIRE

See map p.31 (2)

KEY FIGURES: Charles Dickens; Sir Arthur Conan Doyle
KEY LOCATIONS: Charles Dickens Birthplace Museum; Hawke Street

In February 1812, the great novelist Charles Dickens (shown right) was born at 1 Mile End Terrace (today the Charles Dickens Birthplace Museum, 393 Commercial Road). His father, John, was a clerk in the Navy Pay Office. Money was extremely tight and in June the family had to move to a smaller house at 18 Hawke Street. This has since been demolished. The Dickens stayed there for the next two years until Dickens' father was given a post in London. In 1838 Charles Dickens returned to Portsmouth while writing *Nicholas Nickleby* (1839). In the novel Nickleby and his companion, Smike, appear at the local theatre with the Crummles theatrical company.

Portsmouth also played an important role in the life of Edinburgh-born Sir Arthur Conan Doyle (1859–1930). From 1882 he practised medicine in Southsea, and it is here that he created his legendary detective Sherlock Holmes.

His character was based on Dr Joseph Bell who had taught Doyle medicine at Edinburgh University. Dr Watson, the narrator of the Holmes stories, was based on Doyle's friend Dr James Watson, President of the Portsmouth Literary and Scientific Society.

By the time Doyle left Southsea, he had written several stories featuring Holmes, including *A Study in Scarlet* (1887), and also *Micah Clarke* (1889), *The Sign of Four* (1890) and *The White Company* (1891).

(i) information

Contact details

Portsmouth
Hampshire

☎ +44 (0)2392 826722 (overseas)
023 9282 6722 (UK)

www Tourist Information:
www.visitportsmouth.co.uk

Transport links

Portsmouth Harbour

The M275 off the M27 and the A27 lead straight to Portsmouth

JANE AUSTEN'S HOUSE
HAMPSHIRE

See map p.31 3

KEY FIGURE: Jane Austen
KEY LOCATION: Jane Austen's House Museum

When Jane Austen, her widowed mother and her sister, Cassandra, moved to Chawton Cottage in July 1809, they chose it because it was near Chawton Manor, which was owned by Jane's newly widowed brother, Edward.

It was here that Jane wrote the final versions of her novels. Space was limited so she had to write in the sitting room she shared with her mother and sister, and she would hastily tidy away her papers whenever anyone entered the room – the creaky sitting room door gave her adequate warning of someone's approach.

If the circumstances of Jane's life – living in a small country cottage with her widowed mother and younger sister – sound uncannily like those of the two sisters in *Sense and Sensibility* (1811), it is hardly surprising, as this was the first novel of hers to be published.

▲ *Chawton Cottage, where Jane Austen lived from 1809, is now a museum devoted to her memory.*

More novels followed. *Pride and Prejudice*, which began life as *First Impressions* in 1797, was published in 1813. *Mansfield Park* (1814), *Emma* (1815), *Persuasion* (1818) and *Northanger Abbey* (1818) all were written at Chawton Cottage.

(i) information

Contact details

Jane Austen's House Museum
Chawton
Alton
Hampshire
GU34 1SD

☎ +44 (0)1420 83262

Jane Austen House Museum:
www.jane-austens-house-museum.org.uk

Transport links

🚆 Alton

🚗 The A31 and the A339 pass by Alton

GILBERT WHITE'S HOUSE
HAMPSHIRE

See map p.31 **4**

KEY FIGURES: Gilbert White; Thomas Pennant
KEY LOCATIONS: Gilbert White's House and Garden; Selborne Common

Selborne is synonymous with the naturalist Gilbert White (1720–93), who was born in the vicarage and spent most of his life in the village.

He lived at The Wakes from 1751 until his death. He loved the abundance of nature that he was able to observe in his garden and the surrounding countryside, and this inspired him to begin writing the letters about his observations, which were eventually collected in his book, *The Natural History and Antiquities of Selborne* (1789). The recipients of his letters were two other naturalists, Thomas Pennant and Daines Barrington, and their correspondence began in 1767. Pennant was also an author and his book describing his tours of Scotland, Wales and the Hebrides was published in the 1770s.

After White's death he was buried to the north of the chancel in Selborne churchyard.

The very simple headstone bears only his initials and the date of his death, and can easily be missed. There are two beautiful stained glass windows in the church commemorating White: one depicts St Francis preaching to the birds with representations of every bird mentioned in the book and the other shows the mammals, reptiles, amphibians and insects he wrote about.

The Wakes is now called Gilbert White's House and Garden and the garden is restored to how it would have been in White's time. There is a zig-zag path that leads up to Selborne Common where White did much of his observing.

White was a pioneer of natural history through close observation in the field and his book is considered one of the founding texts of natural history writing. It is also one of the bestselling books of all time in the English language.

ⓘ information

Contact details

Gilbert White's House
Selborne
Alton
Hampshire
GU34 3JH

☎ +44 (0)1420 511275

www Official Museum:
www.gilbertwhiteshouse.org.uk

Transport links

🚊 Alton

🚗 The A31 and the A339 pass by Alton

TENNYSON'S LANE
SURREY

See map p.31 ⑤

KEY FIGURE: Alfred, Lord Tennyson
KEY LOCATIONS: Aldworth; Isle of Wight

By the time Alfred Tennyson (1809–92; shown right) and his wife, Emily, moved to Haslemere in 1869, Tennyson had reached the height of his fame and more modern poets were snapping at his heels. He had been Poet Laureate since 1851, and was a great favourite of Queen Victoria. She felt an especial empathy for him after the death of her husband, Prince Albert, in 1861, when she took great comfort from Tennyson's epic poem, *In Memoriam* (1850), which dealt with his grief following the death of his dear friend, Arthur Hallam.

In 1865, the Tennysons moved to a farmhouse near Haslemere. They had spent many years living at Farringford (now a hotel), in Freshwater on the Isle of Wight, but it was becoming too busy with sightseers who wanted a glimpse of the poet, and from then on they divided their time between the island and Surrey.

The couple bought some land in Surrey and started to build their new home, Aldworth (which was named after Emily's family home in Berkshire) near the summit of Blackdown. Tennyson was able to relax, garden, entertain friends and enjoy family life here. He particularly enjoyed walking around the neighbouring countryside, and Tennyson's Lane is named after him.

Tennyson died at Aldworth in October 1892, having read Shakespeare's *Cymbeline* just a few hours earlier. In tribute, the book was placed in his coffin when he was buried next to many famous poets in Westminster Abbey in London.

ⓘ information

Contact details
Tennyson's Lane
Haslemere, Surrey
GU27 3AF

Transport links
🚆 Haslemere

🚗 The A266 passes through Haslemere

PINEY COPSE

SURREY

See map p.31 (6)

KEY FIGURE: E.M. Forster

KEY LOCATIONS: West Hackhurst; Piney Copse

E.M. Forster had a long-standing affection for the quintessentially English countryside around Abinger in Surrey. This was where he grew up and where his father built a house, West Hackhurst, for his sister, Laura. When Laura died in April 1924 she left the house to Forster.

When Forster learned that the adjoining wood, Piney Copse, was under threat, he bought it. Many of the trees had been felled during the First World War so Forster set about replanting the wood. He opened Piney Copse for the annual treat of the local school and wrote an essay about it, 'My Wood', for the *New Leader* in 1926.

Forster loved West Hackhurst and Piney Copse, but the house was leasehold and the freeholder, Lord Farrer, agreed to renew the lease on the condition that Forster sold him Piney Copse. Forster instead left Piney Copse to the National Trust after his death and lost West Hackhurst.

▲ *Piney Copse was E.M. Forster's beloved stretch of woodland near West Hackhurst.*

(i) information

Contact details

Piney Copse
Abinger
Surrey

National Trust (Piney Copse):
www.nationaltrust.org.uk

National Trust (South-East)
+44 (0)1372 452023

Transport links

Gomshall, Holmwood

The B2127 and B2126 pass by Abinger and the A29 is nearby

ASHDOWN FOREST

EAST SUSSEX

See map p.31 (7)

KEY FIGURE:	A.A. Milne
KEY LOCATIONS:	Poohsticks Bridge; Cotchford Farm

Fans of the stories featuring Winnie-the-Pooh by A.A. Milne (1882–1956) should not have difficulty in recognizing the landscape of Ashdown Forest because it bears such a startling resemblance to Hundred Acre Wood, where Pooh, Piglet and their friends played with Christopher Robin. Here are the lofty Scots pines straight from the illustrations by E.H. Shepard, with their bare trunks topped by little sprouts of green. Here also, if you care to scramble through the woods to find it, is the original Poohsticks Bridge where Pooh and his friends saw Eeyore floating past while they dropped sticks into the river and waited to see whose stick sailed under the bridge first.

A.A. Milne knew the area well because he and his family spent their summer holidays here each year. They stayed at Cotchford Farm, next to Upper Hartfield, and Milne's son – known to his family as Billy Moon but to the rest of the world as Christopher Robin – explored the woods, lanes and sand pits of Ashdown Forest. Christopher Milne's (1920–96) autobiographies are fascinating guides for anyone who wants to discover firsthand the haunts of Winnie-the-Pooh.

Christopher Robin Milne and his teddy bears provided ▷ the inspiration for his father's Winnie-the-Pooh stories.

(i) information

Contact details

Ashdown Forest
Danehill
East Sussex

Ashdown Forest Tourism
Association:
www.ashdownforest.com

Transport links

East Grinstead

The A22 passes by
Ashdown Forest

BRIGHTON
EAST SUSSEX

See map p.31 (8)

KEY FIGURES: Dr Samuel Johnson; Fanny Burney; Charles Dickens; Jane Austen; William Thackeray; Sir Arthur Conan Doyle; Arnold Bennett; W. Somerset Maugham; Graham Greene

KEY LOCATIONS: Bedford Hotel; Old Ship Inn; Brighton Beach

The seaside resort of Brighton was put firmly on the social map at the end of the 18th century when the Prince of Wales, later King George IV (1820–30), visited the town and took a liking to it. It had previously been a fishing village called Brighthelmstone, but with the Prince's patronage it began to go up in the world.

In the 1770s, Hester and Henry Thrale rented a house in West Street for the summer holidays, and their close friend Dr Samuel Johnson began to join them on their annual visits to the Sussex coast. During one trip, Dr Johnson was busy working on *The Lives of the Poets* (1781), one of his great literary achievements. When Johnson was commissioned to write the book, the plan was that he should write biographical prefaces to the selected poems of 52 English poets, but what had been intended to be short prefaces grew into an entire book. It became a massive project. The

▼ In Graham Greene's Brighton Rock, *Hale was murdered by Pinkie while enjoying the delights of the Palace Pier.*

Thrales also entertained Fanny Burney in Brighton. The couple took her to the Assembly Rooms, which were attached to the Old Ship Inn in Ship Street.

The Thrales' house was later knocked down and replaced by a concert hall at which Charles Dickens gave readings. Dickens sometimes lodged at the Old Ship Inn. He also stayed at 62 East Street, 148 Kings Road and at the Bedford Hotel where he wrote parts of *Dombey and Son* (1848). Some of this book is set in Brighton; Mrs Pipchin keeps a children's boarding house where the Dombey children have the misfortune to stay.

Brighton also appears in *Pride and Prejudice* (1813) by Jane Austen; *Vanity Fair* (1848) by William Thackeray (1811–63); *Rodney Stone* (1896) by Sir Arthur Conan Doyle; *Clayhanger* (1910) and *Hilda Lessways* (1911) by Arnold Bennett (1867–1931); *Of Human Bondage* (1915) by W. Somerset Maugham (1874–1965) and, of course, *Brighton Rock* (1938) by Graham Greene (1904–91). Greene's novel concentrated on the seedy side of Brighton, a world of gang warfare, casual sex and emotional cruelty. Greene later painted a happier, breezier side of the town in *Travels with my Aunt* (1969).

ⓘ information

Contact details

Brighton
East Sussex

☎ Tourist Information:
+44 (0)1273 290337

🖥 Tourist Information:
www.visitbrighton.com

Transport links

🚆 Brighton

🚗 The A27 passes by Brighton and the A23 passes through

LEWES
EAST SUSSEX

See map p.31 ⑨

KEY FIGURES:	John Evelyn; William Harrison Ainsworth; Thomas Paine; Leonard Woolf
KEY LOCATIONS:	Southover Grange; White Hart Hotel; Bull House, Round House

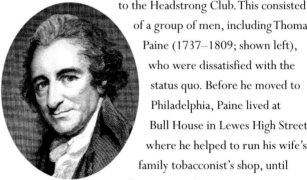

The 17th-century diarist John Evelyn (1620–1706) first came to Lewes when he was a small boy. He stayed with his maternal grandparents, the Stansfields, so he could attend school in the town. In 1630 he attended the Grammar School, which backed onto Southover Grange, the Elizabethan house that was his grandmother's new home after her remarriage following her first husband's death.

Southover Grange was later transformed into Mock Beggars Hall when William Harrison Ainsworth (1805–82) chose it as the setting for his Civil War novel *Ovingdean Grange – A Tale of the South Downs* (1860). The gardens of Southover Grange are still open to the public.

In the 1760s, the upper room in the White Hart Hotel, in Lewes's High Street, was home to the Headstrong Club. This consisted of a group of men, including Thomas Paine (1737–1809; shown left), who were dissatisfied with the status quo. Before he moved to Philadelphia, Paine lived at Bull House in Lewes High Street, where he helped to run his wife's family tobacconist's shop, until they separated.

In July 1919, Leonard Woolf (1880–1969), who had recently bought the Round House in Lewes with his wife, Virginia, attended a house auction at the White Hart. He fell in love with Monk's House in Rodmell, which he bought for £700. They subsequently sold the Lewes house.

ⓘ information

Contact details

Lewes
East Sussex

🖥 Lewes District Council: www.lewes.gov.uk

☎ Tourist Information: +44 (0)1273 483448

Transport links

🚆 Lewes

🚗 The A27 passes by Lewes and the A26 passes through

MONK'S HOUSE
EAST SUSSEX

See map p.31 (10)

KEY FIGURES: Virginia and Leonard Woolf
KEY LOCATIONS: Monk's House; The River Ouse; Charleston Farmhouse

When Virginia and Leonard Woolf bought Monk's House, in Rodmell, it was a simple cottage that lacked a lavatory, bath and hot water. Such privations were soon remedied and the Woolfs established a comfortable domestic routine that Virginia described vividly in her many letters and diaries. Leonard gardened or wrote while Virginia composed her novels such as *The Waves* (1931; shown right) in her garden hut. Virginia embarked on long walks along the banks of the nearby River Ouse, and enjoyed her close proximity to Charleston, the Sussex home of her adored sister, Vanessa.

T.S. Eliot (1888–1965) was one of the first of many visitors to the house. E.M. Forster and Vita Sackville-West (1892–1962), with whom Virginia had an intimate and possibly sexual relationship, were also regulars at the house.

Virginia's physical and mental health was becoming increasingly fragile and led to several breakdowns. Finally, on 28 March 1941 she wrote farewell letters to Leonard and Vanessa, loaded her pockets with stones and drowned herself in the River Ouse. It took three weeks for her body to be found.

Virginia's ashes are buried under one of the two tall elms in the garden at Monk's House. Leonard continued to live and write at Monk's House until his own death in 1969.

(i) information

Contact details

Monk's House
Rodmell
Lewes
East Sussex
BN7 3HF

☎ +44 (0)1323 870001

[www] National Trust:
www.nationaltrust.org.uk/main/
w-monkshouse

Transport links

🚈 Southease

🚗 The A26 and the A27 pass near Rodmell

CHARLESTON FARMHOUSE
EAST SUSSEX

See map p.31 (11)

KEY FIGURES: Virginia Woolf; Vanessa Bell; Duncan Grant; E.M. Forster; Lytton
                     Strachey; David Garnett; John Maynard Keynes; Frances Partridge
KEY LOCATIONS: Charleston Farmhouse; Firle; Monk's House; Lewes

In 1916, the writer Virginia Woolf found what she hoped would be a suitable home for her sister, the painter Vanessa Bell (1879–1961). Although Vanessa was married to Clive Bell at the time, she was living in Suffolk with the painter Duncan Grant (1885–1978), who was anxious to avoid being sent to fight in the First World War. Grant had become a full-time agricultural worker in order to escape conscription, and when he moved with Vanessa to Charleston Farm in Firle, near Lewes, he worked for a neighbouring farmer.

Charleston soon became a popular country retreat for many members of the Bohemian Bloomsbury Group. Made up of many of the leading artists, writers and intellectuals of the time, the Bloomsbury set was extremely influential in all sectors of society. The artists decorated Charleston's walls, doors and furniture, drawing inspiration from Post Impressionist art and Italian fresco painting. The gardens were redesigned based on those found

◄ *The beautiful gardens at Charleston provided the perfect country retreat for the Bloomsbury Group.*

in southern Europe, with gravel paths, mosaics, box hedges and ponds. Vanessa loved the house and garden and wrote that it was: 'most lovely, very solid and simple, with … perfectly flat windows and wonderful tiled roofs. The pond is most beautiful, with a willow at one side and a stone or flint wall edging it all round the garden part, and a little lawn sloping down to it.'

Virginia and her husband, Leonard, lived nearby at Monk's House (see page 43), near Lewes, and the two households, complete with guests, visited each other as often as possible.

Life at Charleston was relaxed and unorthodox, and it attracted such visitors as the art critic Roger Fry (1866–1934), E.M. Forster, Lytton Strachey (1880–1932) and Frances Partridge (1900–2004), who wrote about her visits in her series of memoirs drawn from her diaries. The writer and economist John Maynard Keynes

The painter Vanessa Bell helped decorate Charleston.

(1883–1946), a former lover of Duncan Grant, lived nearby at Tilton Farm with his wife, Russian ballerina Lydia Lopokova (1892–1981).

To outsiders, particularly neighbours, the occupants of Charleston appeared highly unconventional. When Vanessa's daughter, Angelica, was born in 1918, writer and publisher David Garnett, another former lover of Duncan Grant, wrote that he might marry her one day, which he did in 1942 after the death of his first wife, Ray. Angelica Garnett later wrote vividly of her childhood and life at Charleston in her memoir, *Deceived with Kindness* (1984).

Charleston continued to be a thriving artistic and literary community for many years until Duncan Grant died in 1978. The house and gardens are open to the public. It hosts the Charleston Literary Festival each year, which attracts many famous literary names.

ⓘ information

Contact details

Charleston Farmhouse
Firle
Lewes
East Sussex
BN8 6LL

☎ +44 (0)1323 811265

Charleston Farmhouse:
www.charleston.org.uk

Transport links

Berwick
Glynde

The A27 passes through Firle

WHITE COTTAGE
EAST SUSSEX

See map p.31 (12)

KEY FIGURES:	Margerie and Malcolm Lowry
KEY LOCATIONS:	Ripe; The Lamb

In January 1956, Margerie Lowry found White Cottage in Ripe, a tiny village in the maze of country lanes that lie to the east of Lewes. It was exactly what she had been looking for – somewhere peaceful and rural, where her husband, the novelist Malcolm Lowry (1909–57), could try to rebuild his failing life and career, but also near the regular medical help he needed to treat his alcoholism and manic depression.

Malcolm Lowry was desperately trying to pick up the threads of his tattered writing career. After the acclaim for his Mexico-set novel *Under the Volcano* (1947), Lowry struggled to write anything that would be a worthy successor to it.

He was able to write again at Ripe, although it must have helped that he was banned from the local pub, The Lamb. Despite this ban he managed to drink again, something which eventually caused his demise. He died in June 1957, after getting drunk and starting a fight with his wife. Margerie ran to a neighbour to ask for help, but when she returned Lowry was dead. He was buried in the churchyard at Ripe, as was Margerie in 1988, although their graves are not together.

Malcolm Lowry *Under the Volcano*

◀ *Geoffrey Firmin's alcoholism forms the central struggle in Malcolm Lowry's semi-autobiographical novel.*

ⓘ information

Contact details

White Cottage
Channers Lane, Ripe
Lewes
East Sussex, BN8 6AS

Transport links

🚆 Berwick
Glynde

🚗 The A22 and the A27 both pass near Ripe

EASTBOURNE
EAST SUSSEX

See map p.31 (13)

KEY FIGURES: George Orwell; Cyril Connolly; Lewis Carroll; Rumer Godden
KEY LOCATIONS: St Cyprian's School; St John's Road; Lushington Road; Moira House

---

For thousands of holidaymakers, Eastbourne is a place of happiness and relaxation. For the young Eric Arthur Blair, who later wrote as George Orwell (1903–50), it was a place that filled him with dread. He was sent to St Cyprian's, a prep school for boys about which he recounts the cruelty and privations he endured there in his essay 'Such, Such were the Joys'. Writer Cyril Connolly (1903–74) also went to St Cyprian's and wrote about the school in *Enemies of Promise* (1938), renaming it St Wulfric's. Despite this flimsy disguise, the piece provoked a reproachful letter from Mrs Wilkes, the headmistress who was universally known to her charges as Flip.

His childhood experiences did not deter Connolly from moving to Eastbourne in 1968. He bought 48 St John's Road, close to the South Downs, and wrote to a friend 'Eastbourne is heaven'. In 1974 Connolly was buried in Berwick Church, at the foot of the Downs.

Charles Lutwidge Dodgson (1832–98), better known as Lewis Carroll, spent each summer holiday at 7 Lushington Road in Eastbourne between 1877 and 1887. He wrote part of *Through the Looking Glass*, in 1871, while staying at the vicarage in Selmeston, a small village between Eastbourne and Lewes.

Rumer Godden (1907–98), the author of *Black Narcissus* (1939) and *The Greengage Summer* (1958) among other novels, was born in Eastbourne but described the town as 'the most dreadful place'. Her family moved to India shortly after she was born, but in 1920 Rumer and her sisters were sent back to school in England. They were sent to Moira House, a private school for girls, where one of the teachers, Miss Swann, encouraged Rumer to write.

(i) information

Contact details

Eastbourne
East Sussex

Local Information:
www.visiteastbourne.com

+44 (0)871 6630031

Transport links

Eastbourne

The A259 passes through Eastbourne

BATEMAN'S
EAST SUSSEX

See map p.31 **14**

KEY FIGURE: Rudyard Kipling
KEY LOCATIONS: Bateman's; The Elms; Pook's Hill

Rudyard Kipling (1865–1936; shown right) and his wife, Carrie, first visited the 17th-century house Bateman's in 1902. They were looking for peace and quiet and were seeking to escape their house The Elms in Rottingdean, situated on the Sussex coast just east of Brighton. Life there was blighted by the death of their seven-year-old daughter Josephine – and by the ever present tourists who hoped to catch a glimpse of Kipling.

At Bateman's they were able to immerse themselves in the Sussex Weald and Kipling could work undisturbed in his study and continued his prodigious output of stories and poems.

The house's tranquil setting, and what Kipling felt to be its good Feng Shui, inspired some of his greatest works, including *Rewards and Fairies* (1910), which contains the famous poem, 'If', and *Puck of Pook's Hill* (1906). Pook's Hill is visible from the house.

In 1915 tragedy struck once again. The Kiplings' only son, John, was killed in action at the Battle of Loos. After this event, much of Kipling's writing focused on war and its repercussions. The shock of John's death coincided with the onset of a gastric ulcer that eventually killed Kipling in 1936. Carrie died in 1940 and bequeathed Bateman's to the National Trust. It has been kept as it would have been when the Kiplings were alive, and displays the Nobel Prize for Literature that was awarded to the author in 1907.

ⓘ information

Contact details

Bateman's Lane
Burwash
Etchingham
East Sussex
TN19 7DS

☎ +44 (0)1435 882302

💻 National Trust (Bateman's):
www.nationaltrust.org.uk

Transport links

🚂 Etchingham

🚗 The A265 passes through Burwash

LAMB HOUSE AND RYE

EAST SUSSEX

See map p.31 **15**

KEY FIGURES: Henry James; E.F. Benson; Radclyffe Hall; Rumer Godden
KEY LOCATIONS: Lamb House (Garden Room and Green Room); Rye

Henry James (1843–1916) lived in his beloved Lamb House in Rye from 1897 until his death. In the summer he worked in the Garden Room, which stood at right angles to the house, and in the winter he moved inside to the Green Room upstairs. James wrote three of his greatest novels in the house – *The Wings of the Dove* (1902), *The Ambassadors* (1903) and *The Golden Bowl* (1904) – and made it Mr Longdon's home in *The Awkward Age* (1899). James entertained a coterie of literary colleagues here, including fellow novelists H.G. Wells (1866–1946), Rudyard Kipling, Joseph Conrad (1857–1924) and Edith Wharton (1862–1937).

The Garden Room was also a favourite haunt of E.F. Benson (1867–1940), who was a later tenant of Lamb House. He moved here in 1919 and stayed until he died in 1940. Benson drew heavily on Lamb House for his series of novels about Tilling, which was Rye in an almost non-existent disguise. Lamb House became Mallards, the so-called ancestral home of the formidable Miss Elizabeth Mapp, before unwise speculations on the Stock Exchange forced her to relinquish it to her arch rival, Mrs Emmeline Lucas, popularly known as Lucia. In 1935, Benson had a lookout built near the Landgate; a plaque exists today to mark this site. Benson enjoyed mixing with his neighbouring writers, including fellow novelist Radclyffe Hall (1880–1943), who lived with her lover, Una, Lady Troubridge, in the High Street. Rumer Godden lived in Lamb House from 1968–74. By this time, the house was the property of the National Trust. She wrote of her experiences in *A House with Four Rooms* (1989).

ⓘ information

Contact details

West Street
Rye
East Sussex
TN31 7ES

☎ +44 (0)1580 762334

National Trust:
www.nationaltrust.org.uk/main/
w-lambhouse

Tourist Information:
www.visitrye.co.uk

Transport links

🚃 Rye

🚗 The A259 and the A268
pass through Rye

ROMNEY MARSH
KENT

See map p.31 **16**

KEY FIGURES: E. Nesbit; Noël Coward; Russell Thorndike; Reverend Richard Barham
KEY LOCATIONS: Dymchurch; St Mary's Bay; St Mary in the Marsh; The Star Inn;
Warehorne Church

One of the most celebrated residents of the quietly beautiful Romney Marsh was Edith Nesbit (1858–1924), the author of several children's books including that perennial favourite *The Railway Children* (1906). She had first discovered this area of Kent in 1893 when she visited Dymchurch, which was then a quiet little fishing village, and she stayed in various holiday homes there during the next few years.

'Bohemian' is a word that is often applied to Edith because of her rather outré life at a time when most of Britain was clutching its collective skirts and avoiding mention of anything improper. Edith, on the other hand, believed in living life to the full. After the death in 1914 of Hubert Bland, her almost compulsively unfaithful first husband, she married Thomas Terry Tucker in February 1917. Edith called him 'the Skipper' as he had once been the captain of the Woolwich Ferry.

They moved out of London when they found two huts in Dymchurch in the area that was then called Jesson but is now known as St Mary's Bay. The two huts were given suitably nautical names: The Long Boat and The Jolly Boat, and were linked by a passageway called 'the Quarterdeck Gangway'. They referred to the kitchen as 'the Galley' and the Skipper would invite their guests to 'come on board'.

◀ *The quiet beauty and huge skies of Romney Marsh have attracted many writers over the centuries.*

They loved their unusual home and when Edith became terminally ill she told the Skipper that she wanted to be buried under an elm tree, with no memorial stone, in the churchyard at St Mary in the Marsh. The Skipper carved a simple wooden memorial, on the back of which is the one word 'Resting', which marks where she was buried in May 1924. In 1958, 100 years after Edith's birth, a stone tablet in her memory was placed inside the church.

Edith Nesbit was not the only writer on the Marsh during the 1920s. Noël Coward took a house at St Mary in the Marsh with his difficult mother, Violet, for a brief spell in 1921. He wrote one of his first and most controversial plays, *The Vortex*, in a converted stable next to The Star Inn. It was during this sojourn that he met Edith Nesbit, whose books he had always loved, and they became great friends, although Edith made it plain that she was not nearly so keen on Coward's mother, who immediately labelled her 'stuck-up'.

PUFFIN CLASSICS

E. NESBIT

THE
RAILWAY CHILDREN

INTRODUCED BY JACQUELINE WILSON

▲ *The railway near her childhood home in Kent inspired E. Nesbit's classic.*

Romney Marsh used to be a favourite haunt of smugglers, who received brandy and tobacco from France at night. This inspired Russell Thorndike (1885–1972) to write *Dr Syn* (1915) while he was living in a boathouse in Dymchurch. The book tells the story of the Vicar of Dymchurch, a former pirate called Captain Clegg, who becomes the Scarecrow at night to lead a gang of smugglers. The novel was so successful that Thorndike wrote another six. These books were set in the 18th century although there were still smugglers on the Marsh when the Reverend Richard Barham (1788–1845) was vicar of Snargate and Warehorne from 1813–20. He lived in the rectory next to Warehorne church, and later set many of the stories in *The Ingoldsby Legends* (1840) in Kentish villages. Barham boasted of Romney's boggy landscape in his book, proclaiming that the world 'is divided into Europe, Asia, Africa, America and Romney Marsh'.

ⓘ information

Contact details

Romney Marsh
Kent

 Local Guide:
www.romneymarsh.co.uk

Transport links

🚆 Appledone

🚗 A259 passes by Romney Marsh

SANDGATE BAY
KENT

See map p.31 **17**

KEY FIGURE: H.G. Wells
KEY LOCATION: Spade House

After a difficult start in life, when he was apprenticed to a draper, an experience he wrote about in his novel *Kipps* (1905), the fate of Herbert George Wells began to improve. He gained a scholarship to the Normal School of Science in London, where he was taught biology by T.H. Huxley (1825–95), the grandfather of the novelist Aldous (1894–1963). Although Wells left before he was able to take his degree, his enthusiasm for science had been kindled. What seemed like a scholastic failure at the time turned out to be marvellous preparation for his later career as the author of some of the most notable science-fiction novels of the 20th century.

Wells' first novel was *The Time Machine* (1895) and by 1898 he was doing so well that he and his second wife, Catherine, could afford to commission the eminent architect C.F. Voysey (1857–1941) to build Spade House for them

in Sandgate Bay near Folkestone. They lived here until 1909 when they returned to London.

At first Wells worked in the study in the house, and then later moved out to a room in the garden. During his time at Sandgate he wrote *Kipps*, *Tono-Bungay* (1909) and *The History of Mr Polly* (1910). Wells enjoyed a busy social life, which included visiting his friend Henry James at Lamb House (see page 49) in Rye until they fell out over artistic differences. He was also involved in the Fabian Society, which was led by Beatrice and Sidney Webb, with help from George Bernard Shaw. This trio invited Wells to join the society, but then regretted it when he tried to convert it from a debating group for intellectuals to a large pressure group that demanded social reform. Inevitably, Wells' relationship with the Fabians came to a difficult end.

(i) information

Contact details

Sandgate Bay
Sandgate
Folkestone
Kent, CT20

Transport links

Folkestone West
Folkestone Central

A259 passes through Sandgate

ST MARGARET'S BAY
KENT

See map p.31 (18)

KEY FIGURES: Noël Coward; Ian Fleming
KEY LOCATIONS: Goldenhurst Farm; White Cliffs of Dover

Noël Coward's love affair with Kent began in the 1920s when he and his mother rented a house at St Mary in the Marsh. Coward (1899–1973) later moved to Goldenhurst Farm near Aldington, which he owned for 30 years. It was requisitioned by the army during the Second World War, but they failed to notify him when they left. Believing he had no country retreat, Coward bought a house at St Margaret's Bay, which his friend, Kay Norton, was selling.

Coward worked profusely at his new house, named White Cliffs, writing *Ace of Clubs*, *Relative Values*, *Quadrille* and *Nude with Violin*. However, he eventually tired of the maritime bustle and moved back to his beloved Goldenhurst, which he had learned was free, in the early 1950s, passing the lease of White Cliffs to Ian Fleming. In 1956, Coward sold both his London house and Goldenhurst, and moved to Jamaica.

 When he first moved to White Cliffs in St Margaret's Bay, Noël Coward loved the sound of the sea.

(i) information

Contact details

St Margaret's Bay
Dover
Kent, CT15

Transport links

🚆 Dover Priory

🚗 The A258 passes near St Margaret's Bay

CANTERBURY

KENT

See map p.31 19

KEY FIGURES: Geoffrey Chaucer; T.S. Eliot; Daniel Defoe; Jane Austen; Charles Dickens; Mary Tourtel; W. Somerset Maugham; Christopher Marlowe; William Somner; Joseph Conrad; Ian Fleming

KEY LOCATIONS: Canterbury Cathedral; Blackfriars Church; St Martin's Church; King's School; St George's Church; Oswalds; The Duck Inn

In 1170, the Archbishop of Canterbury, Thomas Becket (c.1118–70), was murdered in Canterbury Cathedral by four knights who believed, mistakenly or otherwise, that they were acting on the orders of King Henry II. The site of Becket's assassination became a place of pilgrimage and by the 14th century it was one of the three most popular shrines in the world, the other two being in Rome and Jerusalem.

Geoffrey Chaucer (c.1343–1400), who was a member of the royal household

Murder in the Cathedral *was commissioned for the Cathedral Festival in Canterbury in 1935.*

and later attended Parliament, wrote *The Canterbury Tales* after being inspired by the city.

Becket's murder was the inspiration for T.S. Eliot, who told the story in his poetic drama *Murder in the Cathedral* (1935).

Canterbury has many other literary associations. In 1724, Daniel Defoe (1660–1731) preached at Blackfriars church. He was at the height of his creative powers, having already written *Robinson Crusoe* (1719) and *Moll Flanders* (1722). Jane Austen visited the city to see her brother, Edward, and later often stayed at Goodnestone Park outside Canterbury.

Charles Dickens took great pleasure in visiting Canterbury and, in particular, in giving his visitors a special guided tour around the cathedral. Canterbury also appeared in *David Copperfield*. The title character attended Dr Strong's school in the city, and the ever-optimistic Mr Micawber and his family lodged at the Sun Hotel (now a shop) in Sun Street.

Mary Tourtel (1874–1948), the creator of the cartoon character Rupert Bear who delighted generations of children in his yellow scarf and check trousers, trained at the Sidney Cooper School of Art in St Peter's Street. She was buried in 1948 in the churchyard of St Martin's, which is the oldest parish church in England that is still in constant use.

Canterbury is home to one of the oldest schools in Britain, King's School, which stands close to the cathedral. It has an impressive list of old boys, including W. Somerset Maugham (1874–1965) who may have hated the school when he had to attend it but in later years felt sufficiently generous to endow it with a new library. The Maugham Library contains copies of all his books, as well as the manuscripts for his first and last novels: *Liza of Lambeth* (1897) and *Catalina* (1948) respectively. One of his best-known novels, *Of Human Bondage* (1915), is a *roman-á-clef* in which the central character, Philip Carey, is Maugham. He has a miserable time at his school in Tercanbury, which is Canterbury in very thin disguise. After

▼ Geoffrey Chaucer's The Canterbury Tales *recorded the stories of people making a pilgrimage to Canterbury Cathedral.*

Maugham's death in the South of France in 1965, his ashes were buried beneath a rose bush that grows under the window of the library.

The poet and playwright Christopher Marlowe (1564–93) was born in St George's Street in Canterbury in 1564 and christened in St George's Church. Both buildings were bombed during the Second World War and only the tower of the church remains. Marlowe's famous works include the poem 'The Passionate Shepherd to This Love' (1599) and the play *Dr Faustus* (1604), which were both published posthumously. He died in London during a brawl in a tavern in Deptford.

Another old boy, William Somner (1598–1669), wrote *Antiquities of Canterbury*, the first guide book to Canterbury in 1640. It was the start of the English Civil War and, unfortunately, Somner's book was so informative that it helped the Parliamentarians to invade the city. This must have annoyed Somner, who was a Royalist.

From 1920 until his death four years later, Joseph Conrad lived at the rectory, which is now called Oswalds, near Bishopsbourne Church, outside Canterbury. He wrote many

▲ *After attending King's School, Somerset Maugham studied literature and philosophy in Germany.*

books, including *Lord Jim* (1900), *Nostromo* (1904) and the short story, 'Heart of Darkness' (1902), which later became the basis of the film *Apocalypse Now* (1979). In 1924, his funeral mass was held in St Thomas's Church, Canterbury, and he was buried in Canterbury cemetery.

Ian Fleming (1908–64), who made his name as the creator of the James Bond novels, lived for a short time at Bekesbourne near Canterbury, and wrote *You Only Live Twice* (1964) at The Duck Inn in Pett Bottom.

(i) information

Contact details

Canterbury
Kent

Tourist Information:
www.canterbury.co.uk

+44 (0)1227 378 100

Transport links

Canterbury East
Canterbury West

The A2, A28 and A257
pass near Canterbury.

BROADSTAIRS
KENT

See map p.31 (20)

KEY FIGURE: Charles Dickens
KEY LOCATIONS: Albion Street; Victoria Parade; Fort House; Bleak House

The life and works of Charles Dickens are closely connected with Kent. He particularly liked Broadstairs, and brought his family for at least a month's holiday each summer from 1839 to 1851. Even when he went abroad he had a habit of unfavourably comparing the foreign scenery with Broadstairs.

That first summer, in 1839, the family stayed in Albion Street, in buildings that have now become part of the Albion Hotel. A short distance away, in Victoria Parade, is the Dickens House Museum. This contains exhibits in memory of the author, but it has additional interest because it featured strongly in *David Copperfield* (1850) as the house in which David's aunt, Miss Betsey Trotwood, lived. In the novel, Dickens placed the house in Dover, presumably to protect the privacy of its owner, Miss Mary Pearson Strong.

At Fort House, his later home, Dickens loved watching the sea from the window of his study, which is where he finished writing *David Copperfield*, his favourite and, in many ways, most autobiographical novel. It was here that he also began to plot his next novel, *Bleak House* (1853), after which the house is now named, although the original Bleak House is thought to be in St Albans. The study is also the room in which Dickens wrote an article about Broadstairs in 1851, entitled 'Our English Watering Place'. Coupled with Dickens' celebrity, it helped turn Broadstairs into a popular resort. It was no longer the tranquil refuge that Dickens desired, and he had little option but to go elsewhere for his holidays.

Bleak House is today a museum. Its study was also described in Elizabeth Bowen's novel *Eva Trout* (1968).

 **information**

Contact details

Broadstairs
Kent
CT10

Local Information:
www.visitbroadstairs.co.uk

Transport links

Broadstairs

The A255 passes through Broadstairs

SISSINGHURST CASTLE
KENT

See map p.31

KEY FIGURES:	Vita Sackville-West; Virginia and Leonard Woolf
KEY LOCATIONS:	Garden; South Cottage; Tower; Writing Room

Sissinghurst is famous for its gardens and draws thousands of visitors to its grounds each year. The one-time home of Vita Sackville-West and her husband Harold Nicolson, it is also the site of Vita's famous tower.

Vita wanted to be remembered as a poet and writer, but feared that instead she would remain in the public's collective memory as the gardening correspondent for *The Observer*. Although Vita's gardening work is influential – Vita is a founding member of the National Trust's gardening committee – her work in literature was also recognized and she was made a Companion of Honour for her literary work in 1948.

Her gardening and writing skills reached their zenith at Sissinghurst Castle.

Vita and Harold bought Sissinghurst Castle in 1930, when it was little more than a collection of dilapidated buildings surrounded by fields of cabbages, brambles and rusty sardine tins. Despite such an unprepossessing prospect, the Nicolsons were enchanted and began the long process of turning Sissinghurst into a habitable home. It took five years alone before they had mains water and electricity.

Vita and Harold had already created one garden at their previous home, Long Barn in Weald village, but now they set about creating something on a much larger and more ambitious scale. Harold, who was initially a diplomat and later an MP, was also a writer and journalist; his works include *Some People* (1927) and his three volumes of diaries (1966–68). When not in London, Harold wrote on the ground floor of the South Cottage, while Vita worked in a room halfway up the tower in a different part of the garden.

The tower was Vita's private domain, where she was able to satisfy her innate need for seclusion and reclusiveness, and where she could work on her books and poetry. These included her biography of St Theresa of Avila and St Therese of Lisieux, *The Eagle and the Dove* (1943) and her long poem *The Garden* (1946). Both the tower and the garden were Vita's refuge whenever a love affair became too complicated or when her own chronic shyness and incipient loneliness overwhelmed her.

Very few people were allowed to cross the threshold of Vita's writing room, and her sons, Nigel and Ben, were even forbidden to climb the spiral staircase that led to it. Whenever Vita was wanted for a meal or a telephone call, she was called from the foot of the staircase in the opposite turret: she could not be fetched in person. Even now, the many thousands of visitors who gather at Sissinghurst each year are only allowed to peer through the wrought-iron gate which blocks the doorway of the writing room.

The original printing press with which her friends and publishers Virginia and Leonard Woolf began the Hogarth Press is also on display at the Castle.

▲ *Vita Sackville-West worked in a small room in the tower, to which her family were not allowed access.*

ⓘ information

Contact details

Sissinghurst Castle
Biddenden Road
Near Cranbrook
Kent, TN17 2AB

National Trust (Sissinghurst Castle)
www.nationaltrust.org.uk

☎ +44 (0)1580 710701

Transport links

🚆 Staplehurst

🚗 The A262 passes by Sissinghurst

KNOLE

KENT

See map p.31 (22)

KEY FIGURES: Ben Jonson; John Donne; Vita Sackville-West; Virginia Woolf
KEY LOCATIONS: The King's Bedroom

The first major transformation of Knole was undertaken in 1465 by Thomas Bourchier (c.1406–86), the Archbishop of Canterbury, who spent 30 years of his life restoring the rugged house. It then went through the ownership of four more Archbishops before Henry VIII acquired it and expanded it to a suitably royal size. In 1566 Elizabeth I offered the house to her cousin Thomas Sackville (1536–1608), the 1st Earl of Dorset, and it has remained in the Sackville family ever since. The Sackvilles have many literary associations: Thomas Sackville was a writer, and the 3rd Earl entertained the playwrights Sir Francis Beaumont (1584–1616), John Fletcher (1579–1625) and Ben Jonson (c.1572–1637) and the poet John Donne (1572–1631) here. Donne used to preach in the chapel at Knole each year during his annual visit to his nearby parish church of St Nicholas in Sevenoaks. The 3rd Countess of Dorset was often moved to tears by Donne's sermons.

It was one of the great tragedies in the life of Vita Sackville-West (1892–1962) that her sex prevented her inheriting Knole, which is where she was born and was her beloved childhood home. She was the only child of the 3rd Lord Sackville and, much to her distress, when he died the title and Knole passed to her uncle, Eddy Sackville-West. Vita had always been a tomboy, which made the British rules of primogeniture even harder to bear.

Any child growing up in such an atmospheric old house would be impressed by its scale, beauty and grandeur: the house is said to contain 7 courtyards, representing the days of the week, 52 staircases, for the weeks in the year, and 365 rooms, one for every day of the year. But Knole made a particularly powerful impact on Vita, who had a strong aesthetic sense, a love of history and a powerful imagination. In later life, when she had become established as a poet and novelist (writing as V. Sackville-West), she drew

▼ After it was inherited by her cousin, Vita Sackville-West sometimes took moonlit walks through Knole.

heavily on her memories of Knole. The King's Bedroom, filled with solid silver furniture for a visit from James I of England and left virtually untouched ever since, was where Vita had first been properly kissed by Harold Nicolson (1886–1968), who became her husband, and where she later took other lovers.

In *The Edwardians* (1930), Knole becomes Chevron, and the King's Bedroom is the room where Sebastian tries to seduce the doctor's wife. Vita also wrote a biography of the house, *Knole and the Sackvilles* (1922), into which she was able to pour her love and knowledge of her ancestral home.

The heady combination of Knole and Vita fired the imagination of Virginia Woolf, who was inspired to write *Orlando* (1928) about them both. At the time, the two women were conducting a passionate friendship, and the novel is essentially Virginia's greatest love letter to Vita. It is crammed with incidents and people from Vita's life, and covers four centuries from its Elizabethan beginnings to its end on 11 October 1928, which was the publication day. Virginia gave the manuscript to Vita, who presented it to Knole. The manuscript is still on display in the house today.

ⓘ information

Contact details

Knole
Sevenoaks
Kent, TN15 0RP

☎ +44 (0)1732 450608

National Trust:
www.nationaltrust.org.uk/main/
w-knole

Transport links

🚆 Sevenoaks

🚌 The A224 and the A225 pass through Sevenoaks

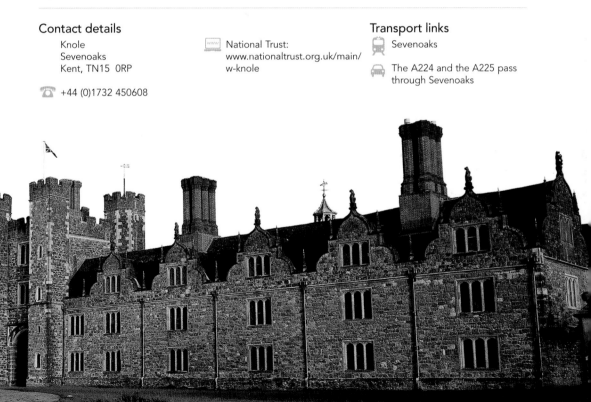

ROCHESTER

KENT

See map p.31 **23**

KEY FIGURES: Charles Dickens; Hans Christian Andersen
KEY LOCATIONS: Rochester Castle; Restoration House; Eastgate House Museum

Charles Dickens knew Rochester well as a boy and, in common with other places in Kent, it inspired many of his novels. In *The Posthumous Papers of the Pickwick Club* (1837), that comic scoundrel, Mr Jingle, describes Rochester Castle in his characteristic, telegraphic style: 'Ah, fine place!... glorious pile – frowning walls – tottering arches – dark nooks – crumbling staircases.' Mr Pickwick stayed at the Bull Hotel, which is now the Royal Victoria and Bull Inn. The streets are crammed with many other reminders of favourite Dickens characters, such as Restoration House in Crow Lane, which was the model for Miss Havisham's cobweb-infested home in *Great Expectations* (1861). Eastgate House Museum in the High Street became the Nun's House – Miss Twinkleton's Seminary for Young Ladies in *The Mystery of Edwin Drood* (1870), in which Rochester is transformed into Cloisterham.

The Swiss chalet in which Dickens wrote several of his later books is now in the garden of Eastgate House. It was originally assembled in the garden at Gad's Hill (now a school), which was Dickens' home from 1856 until his death there in 1870. He had always loved Gad's Hill as a boy and he was able to buy the house in 1856. It was his holiday home until September 1860 when he made it his permanent residence.

One of the first guests in 1856 was Hans Christian Andersen (1805–75), the children's author. However, the visit was not an unparalleled success. Dickens wrote that his family were 'suffering a good deal from Andersen' because it was so difficult to understand what he was saying.

Dickens died on the dining room sofa at Gad's Hill on 9 June 1870, having had a stroke the day before after spending hours writing *Edwin Drood*.

(i) information

Contact details

Rochester
Kent

☎ +44 (0)1634 338141

🌐 Tourist Information:
www.visitmedway.org/site/destination-guide/rochester

Transport links

🚉 Rochester

🚗 The M2 passes by Rochester and the A2 passes through

THE RED HOUSE
BEXLEYHEATH

See map p.31 (24)

KEY FIGURE: William Morris
KEY LOCATION: The Red House

William Morris (1834–96) and his wife Jane Burden (1839–1914) moved to the Red House (shown right) in 1859; it had been built by fellow designer Philip Webb. Morris was at the beginning of his career as a textile and furniture designer and had just published *The Defence of Guenevere and Other Poems* (1858). He had just married Jane who was one of the most popular models for the Pre-Raphaelite painters. Jane later had an affair with Morris's great friend, Dante Gabriel Rossetti (1828–82).

The Morrises lived in the house for five years and it was his failure to find decent furniture that led to him founding the design firm, Morris, Marshall, Faulkener & Co. The Red House remained in private hands until it was acquired by the National Trust and opened to the public in 2003.

(i) information

Contact details

The Red House
Red House Lane
Bexleyheath
Kent, DA6 8JF

☎ +44 (0)20 8304 9878

National Trust:
www.nationaltrust.org.uk/main/
w-redhouse

Transport links

Bexleyheath

The A220 and the A207
pass near to Bexleyheath

LONDON

As Dr Samuel Johnson so famously observed, when you are tired of London you are tired of life. Johnson certainly never grew bored with the city and enjoyed living in Gough Square in the heart of the metropolis. Many writers have spent time in London – some were just passing through, while others made it their home. Some areas of London are associated with particular writers: Hampstead is connected with Keats, even though he spent only a few years there before leaving for Italy in the vain hope of finding a cure for his tuberculosis. Bloomsbury gave its name to the coterie of writers who lived there, including Virginia Woolf and Lytton Strachey. Chelsea is linked with Oscar Wilde, who lived immodestly in Tite Street. Meanwhile, Baker Street conjures up both Sherlock Holmes and his creator, Sir Arthur Conan Doyle.

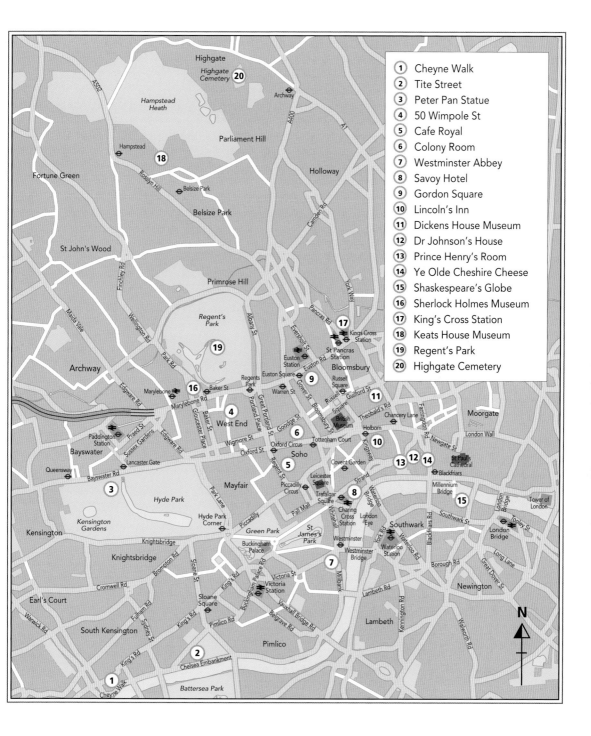

1. Cheyne Walk
2. Tite Street
3. Peter Pan Statue
4. 50 Wimpole St
5. Cafe Royal
6. Colony Room
7. Westminster Abbey
8. Savoy Hotel
9. Gordon Square
10. Lincoln's Inn
11. Dickens House Museum
12. Dr Johnson's House
13. Prince Henry's Room
14. Ye Olde Cheshire Cheese
15. Shaskespeare's Globe
16. Sherlock Holmes Museum
17. King's Cross Station
18. Keats House Museum
19. Regent's Park
20. Highgate Cemetery

CHEYNE WALK

SW3, SW10

See map p.65 **1**

KEY FIGURES: Dante Gabriel Rossetti; George Eliot; Elizabeth Gaskell
KEY LOCATIONS: No. 16; No. 4; No. 93; No. 104; Carlyle Mansions; Chelsea Old Church

---

Cheyne Walk has long been one of London's greatest literary streets and it has been familiar to many writers since the 19th century.

In 1862, Dante Gabriel Rossetti rented No. 16. He was not an ideal neighbour, as he kept peacocks that screeched so loudly that later tenants were legally banned from keeping them. Rossetti stayed here until 1882, during which time the house was the meeting place of many artists and poets. Algernon Swinburne (1837–1909) stayed here from time to time as did George Meredith (1828–1909), who lived round the corner at 8 Hobury Street from 1858–59; Oscar Wilde and William Morris were also frequent visitors to the house.

A drinking fountain in memory of Rossetti stands between Cheyne Walk and the Embankment, with a bronze medallion

LONDON COUNTY COUNCIL

GEORGE ELIOT 1819-1880 NOVELIST died here

of the poet cast by his friend and fellow Pre-Raphaelite, Ford Madox Brown (1821–93), in 1887.

George Eliot moved into 4 Cheyne Walk in early December 1880 with her husband, John Cross. Eliot died of renal failure in the house on 22 December the same year.

The novelist Henry James spent each winter from 1912 at Carlyle Mansions, on the corner of Lawrence Street, and died here in 1916. There is a memorial plaque to him in the churchyard of Chelsea Old Church.

The author Elizabeth Stevenson, who later became known as Mrs Gaskell (1810–65), was born at 93 Cheyne Walk. She spent the first year of her life here until she was taken to Knutsford, Cheshire, which she wrote about in *Cranford* (1853). Hilaire Belloc (1870–1953) and his wife lived at No. 104 from 1901 to 1905.

(i) information

Contact details
Cheyne Walk
Chelsea
London SW3, SW10

Transport links
⊖ Sloane Square
South Kensington

34 TITE STREET
SW3

See map p.65 **2**

KEY FIGURE: Oscar Wilde
KEY LOCATIONS: No. 34; No. 1

Oscar Wilde (1854–1900) lived here from 1885 until his imprisonment in 1895. He already knew the street, having lived at No. 1 for a short time in 1880 with his fellow Oxford graduate, Frank Miles.

Wilde moved back to Tite Street on 1 January 1885 with his pregnant wife, Constance. The couple's son, Cyril, was born at home in June 1885. Their younger son, Vyvyan, was born in November 1886. The house was then No. 16 Tite Street although it is today No. 34.

In order to support his new family, Wilde became editor of *The Woman's World* magazine from 1887 to 1889. He also wrote his most noted plays and books while living here, including *The Happy Prince* (1888), *The Picture of Dorian Gray* (1891), *Lady Windermere's Fan* (1892), *A Woman of No Importance* (1893), *An Ideal Husband* (1895) and *The Importance of Being Earnest* (1895).

▲ *Oscar Wilde cultivated his aesthetic image and believed in 'Art for art's sake'.*

ⓘ information

Contact details
34 Tite Street
Chelsea
London SW3 4JA

Transport links
⊖ Sloane Square

PETER PAN STATUE

KENSINGTON GARDENS, W8

See map p.65 ③

KEY FIGURE: J.M. Barrie
KEY LOCATION: The Long Water, Serpentine River

Peter Pan, the play about the boy who never grew up, was first performed in 1904. It was written by J.M. Barrie (1860–1937), who based it on the stories he used to tell the five boys whose guardian he became after the death of their parents, Arthur and Sylvia Llewellyn Davies. His charges inspired the Lost Boys in the play, whose leader was Peter Pan. Barrie was already a well-known playwright, but the success of *Peter Pan* made him famous. He followed it with *Peter and Wendy*, which was a novelization of the play, in 1911.

Barrie lived in Bayswater Road in West London between 1902 and 1909, and often took his dog, Luath (who became Nana in the play), for a walk in Kensington Gardens. It was here that he first met the Llewellyn Davies boys, so the gardens had very strong emotional and sentimental associations for him. Barrie had the idea for a statue of Peter Pan (shown right) in 1906.

To plan how the statue might look, he took photographs of the young Michael Llewellyn Davies dressed in costume and, in 1912, he commissioned Sir George Frampton (1860–1928) to create the bronze statue. Like an event straight out of Neverland, the statue appeared on the morning of 1 May, having been erected in secret the night before. The statue stands on the west bank of the Long Water (part of the Serpentine River): the place where Peter Pan lands after flying out of his nursery in the story. The statue draws thousands of tourists each year and continues to delight children.

ⓘ information

Contact details

Kensington Gardens
Kensington
London W2 3

🖥 Royal Parks:
www.royalparks.org.uk

Transport links

⊖ Lancaster Gate
Queensway

50 WIMPOLE STREET
W1

See map p.65 (4)

KEY FIGURES: Robert Browning; Elizabeth Barrett Browning
KEY LOCATION: No. 50

In January 1845 Robert Browning wrote a fan letter to Elizabeth Barrett (shown right) who had become a celebrated author after the publication of *The Seraphim, and Other Poems* (1838) and *Poems* (1844). Robert was also making a name for himself, especially after the publication of *Paracelsus* in 1835. Elizabeth admired his work and Robert turned out to be the kindred spirit she had been searching for.

They met for the first time in May 1845. Elizabeth was an invalid who suffered from recurrent chest complaints, which may have been tuberculosis, so she had to receive Browning lying on her sofa in the back room at 50 Wimpole Street. Despite her wan appearance, Browning fell in love with her; he wrote asking her to marry him. Elizabeth was aghast, perhaps even terrified, telling him that he must not mention such things again if he wished to continue to see her. She had good reason to be wary, as her father had convinced himself that none of his 12 children should ever be married. She cast her father as an ogre, who would rather see her 'dead at his foot' than married.

Eventually, the couple decided that the only option was to marry in secret and then elope a short time later. They were duly married on 12 September 1846 and a week later left London. Elizabeth gave birth to their son, Robert, whom they called 'Pen', in March 1849 when she was 43. Elizabeth died in Florence in June 1861.

(i) information

Contact details

50 Wimpole Street
Paddington
London W1G 8

Elizabeth Barrett Browning
Society:
www.browningsociety.org

Transport links

Regent's Park

CAFE ROYAL
64 REGENT STREET, W1

See map p.65 (5)

KEY FIGURES:	Oscar Wilde; Lord Alfred Douglas
KEY LOCATION:	Café Royal

The Café Royal, built in 1885 by the French wine merchant, Daniel Nicols, became a great haunt of many artists and writers. With a lavishly decorated interior (shown right), it was a favourite watering hole of members of the Aesthetic Movement, including the writer Oscar Wilde. His relationship with Lord Alfred Douglas, or 'Bosie' as he called him, took many dramatic twists at the Café Royal. In the autumn of 1892, Bosie's father, the Marquess of Queensberry, became concerned about the nature of the men's relationship. Wilde invited him to lunch at the Café Royal in order to put his mind at rest but, in February 1895, Queensberry confronted Wilde with the truth and Wilde sued for libel.

Wilde hosted another lunch at the Café Royal, this time with Bosie, George Bernard Shaw and Frank Harris (1856–1931), who told Wilde to drop the case. Wilde disagreed and the case came to court. It ended in disaster for Wilde. He was arrested on a charge of gross indecency.

Other habitués included Arnold Bennett (1867–1931), Max Beerbohm (1872–1956), H.G. Wells and Rebecca West (1892–1983).

(i) information

Contact details
Café Royal
68 Regent Street
Westminster
London W1B 5

Transport links
🚇 Piccadilly Circus
Oxford Circus

COLONY ROOM
41 DEAN STREET, W1

See map p.65 6

KEY FIGURES:	Muriel Belcher; Dylan Thomas; Colin MacInnes; Rodney Ackland
KEY LOCATION:	Colony Room

On 15 December 1948, a young woman called Muriel Belcher opened a club on the first floor of 41 Dean Street in the heart of Soho. There were few customers at first, although the Colony Room later became a Mecca for many of the writers and artists for whom Soho was a spiritual home. At the time, in the late 1940s and early 1950s, Soho was a grimy, gritty place where gangsters rubbed shoulders with impoverished artists, such as Francis Bacon (1909–92) and Lucian Freud (1922–2011), and with writers, such as Keith Waterhouse (1929–2009), Dan Farson (1927–97) and Dylan Thomas (1914–53).

Muriel Belcher was renowned for her filthy language and extreme rudeness. One customer whose rudeness was equal to hers was Colin MacInnes (1914–76), the author of *City of Spades* (1957) and *Absolute Beginners* (1959). Both books championed the black cause long before it became fashionable. MacInnes, who delighted in being a member of rackety Soho, was profoundly embarrassed by his mother, who was the novelist, Angela Thirkell (1890–1961). He described her as 'an immensely successful and bad writer'.

It was difficult to get into the Colony Room because Muriel Belcher was very careful to weed out the people she considered boring. However, theatregoers who were unable to visit the club in person could visit it vicariously after Rodney Ackland wrote the play *Absolute Hell* (1987), where the action took place in a club named La Vie en Rose, which was obviously the Colony. In the play it was presided over by a woman, Christine Foskett, who was clearly based on Muriel Belcher. The play, which was well received, was a reworking of his earlier play, *The Pink Room* (1952).

(i) information

Contact details

Colony Room
41 Dean Street
Soho
London W1D 4PY

Colony Room:
www.colonyroom.com

+44 (0)20 7437 9179

Transport links

Tottenham Court Road
Piccadilly Circus
Leicester Square

WESTMINSTER ABBEY

SW1

See map p.65 (7)

KEY FIGURES: Geoffrey Chaucer was the first literary figure to be buried here in 1400
KEY LOCATION: Poets' Corner

In the south transept of Westminster Abbey is an area that is now known as Poets' Corner. Geoffrey Chaucer was the first poet to be buried here in 1400. Edmund Spenser (*c.*1552–99), author of *The Faerie Queen* (1590), was buried near Chaucer, thereby unwittingly instigating a tradition that has continued ever since.

Literary celebrity has never been an automatic passport to commemoration in Poets' Corner. George Eliot was excluded from Poets' Corner and buried in Highgate Cemetery instead, although there is a memorial stone in Poets' Corner to mark the centenary of her death. Charles Dickens's celebrity led the public to demand his burial here, even though he would have preferred Rochester.

Other writers buried here include: John Dryden, Dr Johnson, Richard Brinsley Sheridan, Tennyson, Robert Browning, John Masefield, Thomas Hardy and Rudyard Kipling. Some only have memorials, including William Shakespeare, John Milton, the Brontë sisters, Oliver Goldsmith, John Ruskin, Samuel Butler, Robert Burns, Thomas Gray, William Wordsworth, Percy Bysshe Shelley – whose scandalous life meant that he was only given a memorial in 1969 despite having died in 1822 – Sir Walter Scott, William Blake, Henry James, T.S. Eliot, Gerard Manley Hopkins and Sir John Betjeman.

(i) information

Contact details

Westminster Abbey
20 Dean's Yard
Westminster
London SW1P 3PA

Westminster Abbey:
www.westminster-abbey.org

Transport links

St James Park
Westminster

 +44 (0)20 7222 5152

SAVOY HOTEL
WC2

See map p.65 **8**

KEY FIGURES: Oscar Wilde; Arnold Bennett
KEY LOCATION: Savoy Hotel

'My bill here is 49 pounds for a week. I have also got a new sitting-room over the Thames.' So wrote Oscar Wilde to Lord Alfred Douglas in March 1893, while their romance was at its height and before the full weight of outraged Victorian morality descended on Wilde's head (see page 70). During Wilde's subsequent trial in 1895, witnesses were called who testified that he had taken them to his second-floor sitting room at the Savoy for drinks, and later to his bedroom for sex.

Even then the Savoy Hotel was a byword for luxury, and this connection was emphasized by its name, which referred to the old Savoy Palace that had once stood on this spot. The luxurious nature of the hotel made a huge impression on Arnold Bennett when he was taken here for tea at the turn of the 20th century, and inspired him to write *The Grand Babylon Hotel* (1902), which was patently about the Savoy. Bennett was fascinated by large organizations and for many years delighted in discovering what went on behind the scenes at the Savoy. He had privileged access because by now he was a director of the hotel. In 1927, Bennett was treated to a guided tour of the labyrinthine service departments that ensure the smooth running of the Savoy, and the knowledge that he gained was invaluable when he came to write *Imperial Palace* (1930), which was also a thinly disguised Savoy.

This literary connection is still remembered at the Savoy. The dish 'Omelette Arnold Bennett', which is made with smoked haddock and Parmesan cheese, was named for the novelist and continues to appear on the menu.

(i) information

Contact details

Savoy Hotel
Strand
London WC2R 0EU

🖥 Savoy Hotel:
www.fairmont.com/savoy

Transport links

Charing Cross
Embankment
Covent Garden

☎ +44 (0)20 7836 4343

GORDON SQUARE
WC1

See map p.65 ⑨

KEY FIGURES:	Sir Leslie Stephen; Bloomsbury Group
KEY LOCATIONS:	46 and 51 Gordon Square

In the 1920s, Gordon Square was the nerve centre of the literary and artistic set that became known as the Bloomsbury Group after the area of London in which they lived. The epicentre round which they revolved was 46 Gordon Square, the home of the children of Sir Leslie Stephen who was the first editor of the *Dictionary of National Biography*. Thoby, Adrian, Virginia and Vanessa Stephen grew up at 22 Hyde Park Gate, but moved to Gordon Square after their father's death in 1904. They began to entertain their friends on Thursday evenings, and soon their rooms were full of such people as Leonard Woolf, Clive Bell and Lytton Strachey. After Thoby died from typhoid in 1906, Vanessa decided to marry Clive Bell, and Virginia and Adrian moved to 29 Fitzroy Square.

Lytton Strachey, who was one of the central figures of the Bloomsbury Group until his death from stomach cancer in 1932, moved to 51 Gordon Square with his family in 1909 and stayed here until 1917. He became a noted essayist, and his books include *Eminent Victorians* (1918) and *Queen Victoria* (1921).

ⓘ information

Contact details
Gordon Square
Camden
London WC1H

Transport links
⊖ Euston
  Euston Square

LINCOLN'S INN
WC2

See map p.65 (10)

KEY FIGURES: John Donne; Samuel Pepys; John Forster; Charles Dickens
KEY LOCATIONS: Lincoln's Inn; Lincoln Inn Fields; Old Square; New Square

Lincoln's Inn, one of the four Inns of Court, was established in the 14th century and began its life as a thriving community of lawyers-in-training. Many plays were put on here for the student audience during the Renaissance and Restoration periods. Poet and priest John Donne entered the Inn in 1592, and shared rooms with a fellow poet, Christopher Brooke. Donne was later to become the first Chaplain of the Inn's chapel. Samuel Pepys wrote in his famous diaries about plays that he'd seen at Lincoln's Inn. Other literary members of the Inn include Lord Macaulay (1800–59), best known for the *History of England* (1849–61); Thomas Hughes (1822–96), who wrote *Tom Brown's Schooldays* (1857); H. Rider Haggard (1856–1925), author of *King Solomon's Mines* (1885); and John Galsworthy (1867–1933), of *The Forsyte Saga* (1906–21) fame.

Nearby Lincoln's Inn Fields, the largest public square in London today, also has very strong literary connections. It was laid out by Inigo Jones (1573–1652) in 1618. John Forster, who became the hagiographer of his great friend, Charles Dickens, had chambers at No. 58. Forster's house became the home of Mr Tulkinghorn in *Bleak House* (1853).

Dickens knew this area well. When he was 14, he was a solicitor's clerk in New Square. He later used his experiences in books such as *The Posthumous Papers of the Pickwick Club* (1837). Mr Pickwick visits his leading counsel, Serjeant Snubbin, there when he is being sued by Mrs Bardell.

When Dickens wrote *Bleak House*, the Court of Chancery met at Lincoln's Inn, so it became the setting for the case of Jarndyce v. Jarndyce around which the book revolves. The offices of Kenge and Carboy solicitors are in Old Square. Krook's Rag and Bottle Warehouse, where Krook apparently became a case of spontaneous combustion, is in Chichester Rents, near New Square.

(i) information

Contact details

Lincoln's Inn Fields
Holborn
London WC2

Lincoln's Inn:
www.lincolnsinn.org.uk

☎ +44 (0)20 7405 1393

Transport links

⊖ Holborn

DICKENS HOUSE MUSEUM
48 DOUGHTY STREET, WC1

See map p.65 (11)

KEY FIGURE: Charles Dickens
KEY LOCATION: 48 Doughty Street

The Dickens family came up in the world when they moved to 48 Doughty Street in the spring of 1837. They had previously lived in rooms at 15 Furnival's Inn, but now they could afford a prosperous middle-class road, which was closed off at each end and attended by porters wearing mulberry livery. The household consisted of Dickens; his wife, Catherine; Charles, their baby son; and Dickens's brother, Fred.

In 1837, Dickens's star was on the rise. *The Posthumous Papers of the Pickwick Club* had been running as a serial for a year and was starting to make his name. However, very soon after the family moved to Doughty Street their happiness was shattered by the sudden death of 17-year-old Mary Hogarth, Catherine's sister and a frequent visitor to the house. Dickens was so bereft that he had to stop work on *Pickwick Papers* and *Oliver Twist* (1838), which had just begun to appear in monthly instalments. He later used the experience of Mary's death when writing about the demise of Little Nell in *The Old Curiosity Shop* (1841).

Dickens named his eldest daughter, who was born in Doughty Street in March 1838, after Mary. His second daughter, Kate, was born here in October 1839. Two months later, the Dickens family moved from Doughty Street to 1 Devonshire Terrace in Regent's Park.

Dickens was always a prolific writer, even later in life when his prodigious output damaged his health. During his tenure at Doughty Street, he wrote the last five monthly instalments of *Pickwick Papers*, all of *Oliver Twist* except the first five instalments, the whole of *Nicholas Nickleby* (1839), the first few pages of *Barnaby Rudge* (1841) and several shorter pieces.

(i) information

Contact details

The Dickens House Museum
48 Doughty Street
London WC1N 2LX

☎ +44 (0)20 7405 2127

Dickens House Museum:
www.dickensmuseum.com

Transport links

⊖ Russell Square

DR JOHNSON'S HOUSE
17 GOUGH SQUARE, EC4

See map p.65 (12)

KEY FIGURE: Dr Samuel Johnson
KEY LOCATION: 17 Gough Square

In 1746, Dr Samuel Johnson agreed to write what would be the first dictionary of the English language. He worked on the dictionary for nine years, with the help of six assistants.

Johnson was paid an advance of £1,575 for compiling the dictionary, and used the money to rent this house in Gough Square. It was the first time he had known any sort of financial security, although it did not last and throughout his life he had periods in which he struggled to make ends meet. When his mother died he could not pay for her funeral, so in order to raise the required funds he dashed off his novel *Rasselas* (1759) in less than a week.

Johnson and his helpers worked on the dictionary in the attic at Gough Square (shown right), which is now open to the public. He lived here from 1749 to 1759, and the house is the only one of his London homes

to have survived to the present day. It contains portraits of Johnson and his helpers, as well as a first edition of the dictionary, published in 1755.

(i) information

Contact details

Dr Johnson's House
17 Gough Square
London EC4A 3DE

☎ +44 (0)20 7353 3745

🖥 Dr Johnson's House:
www.drjohnsonshouse.org

Transport links

⊖ Temple
Chancery Lane

🚆 City Thameslink

PRINCE HENRY'S ROOM

17 FLEET STREET, EC4

See map p.65 **13**

KEY FIGURE:	Samuel Pepys
KEY LOCATION:	Prince Henry's Room

Prince Henry's Room (shown right) is on the first floor of a Jacobean house in Fleet Street and is dedicated to the life and work of Samuel Pepys. It is one of the ironies of Pepys's life that the one book he deliberately wrote for publication, *Memoires Relating to the State of the Royal Navy in England* (1690), sank into obscurity, while his diaries, which he wrote purely for pleasure, continue to be in print more than 300 years after he wrote them. Pepys recorded every detail of his life, from what he ate to his rows with his wife, and also vividly described what turned out to be a very eventful decade in London's history, with the restoration of Charles II to the throne in 1660, the Great Plague of London in 1665 and the Great Fire of London in 1666. He only stopped writing his diary, in 1669, because he wrongly feared that he was going blind.

ⓘ information

Contact details

Prince Henry's Room
17 Fleet Street
City of London
London EC4Y 1AA

Official Government website
(Prince Henry's Room):
www.cityoflondon.gov.uk

Transport links

Temple

City Thameslink

YE OLDE CHESHIRE CHEESE

WINE OFFICE COURT, EC4

See map p.65 **14**

KEY FIGURES:	Dr Samuel Johnson; Oliver Goldsmith; Charles Dickens
KEY LOCATION:	Fleet Street

This pub, which is situated just off Fleet Street, can rightly claim to be 'olde', as the sign that hangs outside it acknowledges that it was 'rebuilt in 1667'. It was here that Dr Samuel Johnson retreated whenever his writing became too much for him. Johnson once made the heartfelt statement that 'there is nothing which has yet been contrived by man by which so much happiness is produced as by a good tavern or inn'.

Another writer who enjoyed relaxing in Ye Olde Cheshire Cheese was Oliver Goldsmith, who lodged in Wine Office Court while he was writing *The Vicar of Wakefield* (1766). Goldsmith and Johnson met in 1761, and the former became one of the founding members of Johnson's literary group, The Club.

The youthful Charles Dickens used to walk up and down Fleet Street, pressing his nose to the windows of food shops in the vain hope that the sight of food would somehow satisfy his empty stomach. Once he began to earn money, he used to drink in Ye Olde Cheshire Cheese, and undoubtedly enjoyed soaking up the historic atmosphere too. His portrait, as well as those of Johnson and Goldsmith, hangs on the wall, and there is a plaque in his memory. One of the establishment's most famous traditions was to serve an extremely hefty pudding on the first Monday of October; apparently Dickens liked to be the person to make the first incision before it was served to all the diners.

In 1891, the pub became the headquarters of a group of poets calling themselves the Rhymers' Club. They met in the pub for a couple of years to read their poetry, and included W. B. Yeats (1865–1939) and Arthur Symons (1865–1945).

(i) information

Contact details

Ye Olde Cheshire Cheese
145 Fleet Street
Wine Office Court
London EC4A 2BU

☎ +44 (0)20 7353 6170

Transport links

⊖ Chancery Lane
Temple

🚋 City Thameslink

YE OLDE CHESHIRE CHEESE **79**

SHAKESPEARE'S GLOBE

NEW GLOBE WALK, SE1

See map p.65 (15)

KEY FIGURES: William Shakespeare; Sam Wanamaker
KEY LOCATIONS: Bankside; Blackfriars Theatre

In 1989, workmen began building the new Globe Theatre at Bankside. The original, built by the brothers Cuthbert and Richard Burbage in 1598–99, had once stood 200 yards away.

Strongly associated with the English playwright William Shakespeare (shown opposite), the original Globe was famous for the performances of his plays. Shakespeare was a shareholder of the Globe as well as an actor in his plays. He belonged to a troupe of players known as the Lord Chamberlain's Men, which was the biggest theatre company in London at that time.

▼ *The original Globe Theatre was made using the dismantled timber of another playhouse, called The Theatre, located in Shoreditch. The Theatre was dismantled overnight in secret, while its landlord was out of town.*

Globe Theatre, Bankside.

They moved to the Globe after it was completed in 1599 and then, with great political foresight, changed their name to the King's Men in 1603 when James I succeeded to the throne. They could only act at the Globe in the summer, because of its open roof, and from 1608 they began to play winter seasons at the nearby Blackfriars Theatre.

During a performance of *Henry VIII* in 1613, two cannons were fired as usual but a spark from one of them flew up and set the Globe's thatch alight. The theatre burned to the ground, but was rebuilt with the help of public subscriptions and was back in business the following year. After years of successful performances, the Globe was destroyed during the English Civil War in 1644.

For centuries the Globe's remains lay unwanted beneath the South Bank, but in 1949 the theatre director, Sam Wanamaker (1919–93), father of actor Zoe Wanamaker, conceived the notion that he would like to find it again. It was a project that occupied him, off and on, for the rest of his life and which ended with the triumphant creation of Shakespeare's Globe Theatre. The new Globe Theatre is as close to the original in appearance as possible, the only differences being those required by modern safety

laws. Like the original Globe, the theatre has a thatched roof – the first such roof to exist in central London since the Great Fire in 1666 – while the yard at the front of the stage is exposed to the elements.

The new theatre performs Shakespeare's plays, just as the old one did. A complete list of the plays performed at the original Globe does not exist, but it is known that the following were definitely staged here: *Love's Labours Lost*, *The Taming of the Shrew*, *King Lear*, *Macbeth*, *Pericles*, *Othello*, *Romeo and Juliet*, *Henry VIII* and *The Winter's Tale*.

ⓘ information

Contact details

Shakespeare's Globe
21 New Globe Walk
Bankside
SE1 9DT

☎ +44 (0)20 7902 1400

Shakespeare's Globe:
www.shakespearesglobe.com

Transport links

Mansion House
London Bridge

Bankside Pier

THE SHERLOCK HOLMES MUSEUM

239 BAKER STREET, NW1

See map p.65 (16)

KEY FIGURE: Sir Arthur Conan Doyle
KEY LOCATIONS: 239 Baker Street; Montague Place; 2 Devonshire Place

Sir Arthur Conan Doyle's character Sherlock Holmes has become so entwined in popular culture that it is a common misconception that he once walked the streets of London. The first Holmes novel, *A Study in Scarlet*, was published in 1887 and was followed by several short stories that appeared in *The Strand Magazine*. Doyle lived in Montague Place, W1, in 1890 and was trying to practise as an oculist at 2 Devonshire Place, but he could not attract any patients. He soon devoted more attention to writing, which nourished his finances and brought about fame. He swiftly wrote books on a variety of topics, including fairies and spiritualism.

Any Sherlock Holmes fan looking for 221B Baker Street, where Sherlock Holmes lived and was cared for by his housekeeper, Mrs Hudson, will imagine that they have found it when they see the sign on the door at this address. Actually, this building is No. 239, and calling it 221B simply sets the scene. The real 221 Baker Street is the home of the Santander bank.

◄ *This poster is for the 1939 film, The Adventures of Sherlock Holmes, starring Basil Rathbone in the title role.*

(i) information

Contact details

The Sherlock Holmes Museum
239 Baker Street
London NW1 6XE

The Sherlock Holmes Museum:
www.sherlock-holmes.co.uk

☎ +44 (0)20 7224 3688

Transport links

⊖ Baker Street

PLATFORM 9¾
KING'S CROSS STATION
KING'S CROSS, N1

See map p.65 **17**

KEY FIGURE: J.K. Rowling
KEY LOCATION: Platform 9¾

Probably one of the most famous children's book characters created in the latter part of the 20th century is J.K. Rowling's Harry Potter. In the books, at the beginning of each school year, Harry and his schoolmates go to King's Cross station to the stretch of wall inbetween platforms 9 and 10 that leads to their platform. They have to rush at the magical wall with their trolleys to get through to the wizard version of King's Cross.

At the real King's Cross station, visitors will find a trolley buried into a wall and a plaque where platform 9¾ is meant to be located, oddly enough between platforms 8 and 9. Platforms 9 and 10 are in a different building from the main station and also they are adjacent so there is no wall separating them through which students

▲ *Platform 9 3/4 is the magical platform from which young students travelled to their school, Hogwarts.*

would travel. Rowling later admitted her mistake in a BBC interview, saying that, 'I wrote Platform 9¾ when I was living in Manchester, and I wrongly visualized the platforms, and I was actually thinking of Euston [station]'.

ⓘ information

Contact details

King's Cross Station
Euston Road
London N1 9AL

National Rail:
www.nationalrail.co.uk/
stations/KGX.html

Transport links

King's Cross; St Pancras

King's Cross; St Pancras

KEATS HOUSE MUSEUM
10 KEATS GROVE, NW3

See map p.65 (18)

KEY FIGURE: John Keats; Fanny Brawne
KEY LOCATION: 10 Keats Grove

In 1818, John Keats (1795–1821; shown right) was just beginning his career as a poet. He had abandoned his training as a surgeon in 1816 so he could concentrate on poetry instead, and his first volume of poems was published in 1817. His work had its detractors, chiefly in the writer John Lockhart (1794–1854) who wrote some scathing attacks on Keats.

In 1818 Keats went to live with his friend, Charles Armitage Brown (1787–1842), in Hampstead. The semi-detached house was called Wentworth Place; the two houses were converted into one building in the 1830s and later renamed Keats House. The Brawne family lived next door and Keats soon fell in love with the young daughter, Fanny. Both personally and artistically, the following two years were the greatest of Keats' life. He wrote many of his most enduring and best-loved poems, such as 'The Eve of St Agnes', 'Ode to a Nightingale', which it is claimed he wrote after sitting under a plum tree in the front garden of the house, and 'Ode on a Grecian Urn'.

Keats and Fanny became engaged, but the young poet soon realized that he was becoming ill with tuberculosis. After Keats first coughed up blood in his bed, he told his friend, Charles, 'that drop of blood is my death warrant'. The only solution was for Keats to leave the damp, sooty air of England and go to Italy in the hope that the warmer climate would cure him, but he died in Rome in February 1821, at the age of 25.

ⓘ information

Contact details

Keats House
10 Keats Grove
London NW3 2RR

☎ +44 (0)20 7332 3868

Keats House:
www.keatshouse.cityoflondon.gov.uk

Transport links

⊖ Hampstead
Belsize Park

🚆 Hampstead Heath

REGENT'S PARK
NW1

See map p.65 **19**

KEY FIGURES: H.G. Wells; Edmund Gosse; Elizabeth Bowen; W.B. Yeats; Sylvia Plath
KEY LOCATIONS: Hanover Terrace; Clarence Terrace; Primrose Hill

To the visitor, London can feel like one giant city but, as anyone who has lived here knows, it is really a collection of villages. Each has its own flavour and Regent's Park is no exception.

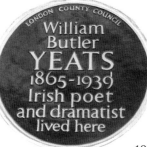

The writer H.G. Wells spent the last few years of his life at 13 Hanover Terrace, from 1937 until his death here in 1946. It was while living here that he wrote his last book, *Mind at the End of its Tether* (1945), which expressed his despair at the prospect of another world war. From 1850 to 1859, Wilkie Collins (1824–89) lived close by at No. 17 with his mother and brother. It was during this interlude that he began to write for Charles Dickens's *Household Words*, and started his thriller *The Woman in White* (1860). Edmund Gosse (1849–1928), the poet and biographer, lived in the same house from 1901 to 1928 and wrote *Father and Son* (1907), which records his difficult relationship with his father.

Elizabeth Bowen (1899–1973) lived at 2 Clarence Terrace from 1935 to 1952. She wrote several novels while here, including *The Death of the Heart* (1938).

Primrose Hill lies to the east of Regent's Park and has also had some literary residents. These include W.B. Yeats, who lived with his family at 23 Fitzroy Road from 1867 to 1874; a blue plaque commemorates his residency (see plaque, above). Poet Sylvia Plath (1932–63) committed suicide in that same house. The writer Kingsley Amis (1922–95) also lived in Primrose Hill, in Regent's Park Road, and used to drink in the Queen's Pub.

ⓘ information

Contact details
Regent's Park
London NW1

Transport links
Regent's Park
Baker Street
Great Portland Street

HIGHGATE CEMETERY

N6

See map p.65 **20**

KEY FIGURES: George Eliot; Sir Leslie Stephen; Dante Gabriel Rossetti
KEY LOCATION: Swains Lane

Highgate Cemetery in north London is one of the greatest 'garden' cemeteries in England and one of the Magnificent Seven (the seven largest cemeteries in London). It consists of two cemeteries that lie on either side of Swains Lane: the West Cemetery, which opened in 1839, and the East Cemetery, which opened in 1854.

This was where many members of the great, the good and sometimes the not-so-good were buried, and it was highly sought-after as the final resting place of wealthy Victorians. However, its fortunes dwindled when its plots filled up and parts of it are now highly atmospheric examples of Victorian sentimentality at its best.

▼ *Many famous people are buried in Highgate Cemetery, including Karl Marx and George Eliot.*

Many Victorian authors who achieved fame were either buried in Westminster Abbey or, if they were refused permission or did not wish the Abbey to be their resting place, in Highgate Cemetery. George Eliot, the female novelist whose life was considered outrageous, was buried in the East Cemetery in 1880. Her married lover, the writer G.H. Lewes, had been buried in the cemetery two years before. Sir Leslie Stephen, who was another Victorian man of letters and the father of Vanessa Bell and Virginia Woolf, was buried in the East Cemetery in 1904.

The death of a loved one sometimes brings out the worst in their relatives, so it is hardly surprising that there are controversies and scandals connected with Highgate Cemetery. When Elizabeth Siddal, who was the wife of Dante Gabriel Rossetti and the favourite model of the Pre-Raphaelite painters, committed suicide in 1862 she was buried in the Rossetti family vault in the West Cemetery. Distraught with remorse at the way he had treated her during their marriage, her husband buried the only manuscript of his love poems with her. Seven years later, however, times were hard for Rossetti and he began to think longingly of those buried

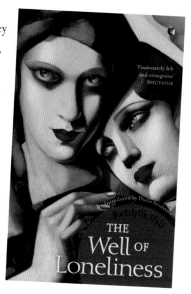

poems and the money they could earn him, so he arranged to have his wife's coffin exhumed. It appears that when her coffin was opened, Rossetti was shocked to discover that her long auburn hair had continued to grow after her death. Rossetti's sister, the poet Christina (1830–94), was also buried in the family tomb, but was allowed to rest there undisturbed. The mournful setting matches the mood of some of her more melancholy poetry.

Other literary figures who were buried here include Frederick Warne, who was Beatrix Potter's publisher; Mrs Henry Wood (1814–87), whose first novel *East Lynne* (1861) was a Victorian bestseller; Stella Gibbons (1902–89), who is chiefly remembered for her first novel, *Cold Comfort Farm* (1932); and Radclyffe Hall, the author of *The Well of Loneliness* (1928; shown above).

ⓘ information

Contact details

Highgate Cemetery
Swain's Lane
London N6 6PJ

☎ +44 (0)20 8340 1834

🖳 Highgate Cemetery:
www.highgate-cemetery.org

Transport links

⊖ Archway
Highgate

EAST ANGLIA

The flat fenland counties of East Anglia have a particular
atmosphere that comes through very strongly in the books
that have links with this part of England. They have a mysterious
quality that may explain why so many crime and thriller writers
have been attracted to the region. Many classic detective
novelists have lived in and written about East Anglia, including
Margery Allingham, Dorothy L. Sayers and P.D. James. Dick
Francis got to know Newmarket during his career as a jockey,
and then created an even more successful career by writing
many thrillers connected with horse-racing, which is romantically
known as 'the sport of kings'. The city of Cambridge offers
another aspect of East Anglia, with its beautiful old colleges
and associations over the centuries with many important
writers, poets and novelists.

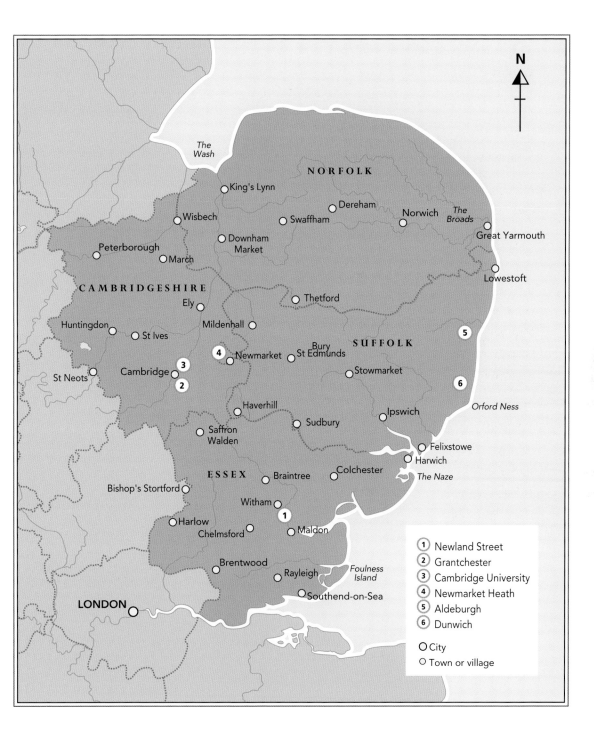

N

The Wash

NORFOLK

King's Lynn

Dereham

Wisbech

Swaffham

Norwich

The Broads

Downham Market

Great Yarmouth

Peterborough

March

Lowestoft

CAMBRIDGESHIRE

Ely

Thetford

Huntingdon

St Ives

Mildenhall

④

SUFFOLK

⑤

③

Newmarket

Bury St Edmunds

Cambridge

Stowmarket

② ⑥

St Neots

Orford Ness

Haverhill

Ipswich

Saffron Walden

Sudbury

Felixstowe

Harwich

ESSEX

Braintree

Colchester

The Naze

Bishop's Stortford

Witham

①

Harlow

Chelmsford

Maldon

Brentwood

Foulness Island

Rayleigh

LONDON

Southend-on-Sea

① Newland Street
② Grantchester
③ Cambridge University
④ Newmarket Heath
⑤ Aldeburgh
⑥ Dunwich

○ City
○ Town or village

NEWLAND STREET

ESSEX

See map p.89 (1)

KEY FIGURE: Dorothy L. Sayers
KEY LOCATIONS: No. 24; No. 18

Although Dorothy L. Sayers (1893–1957) made her name as a very successful author of detective novels featuring her urbane sleuth, Lord Peter Wimsey, later she considered that the medieval and religious subjects that gripped her were much more worthy of her time and effort. These included her play *The Man Born to be King* (1943) and her translations of Dante's *Inferno* (1940) and *Purgatorio* (1953).

Dorothy was born in Oxford and attended Somerville College, where she studied medieval literature. She wrote novels in order to earn a living and after *Whose Body?* was published in 1923, she became one of the greatest exponents of the classic 20th-century detective novel. After a spell in London in an advertising agency, which gave her all the background she needed when she came to write *Murder Must Advertise* in 1933, she moved to Witham in Essex in 1929, where she lived at 24 Newland Street until her death in 1957. A blue plaque (shown left) marks her residency and a statue dedicated to the writer stands outside the library at 18 Newland Street, which contains the Dorothy L. Sayers Centre.

Although Lord Peter's cases took him all over the country, two of the novels that featured the aristocratic detective were set in East Anglia. *The Nine Tailors* (1934) contains highly evocative descriptions of the Fens and some of the old churches there, while *Busman's Honeymoon* (1937) is set in an old East Anglian house where Lord Peter and his wife, writer Harriet Vane, spend their honeymoon while managing to solve a murder at the same time.

Dorothy L Sayers 1893–1957 novelist theologian & Dante scholar lived here

(i) information

Contact details

Dorothy L. Sayers Centre
Witham Library,
18 Newland Street
Witham
Essex, CM8 2AQ

[www] Dorothy L. Sayers Society:
www.sayers.org.uk

Transport links

Witham

From Chelmsford, follow road from A12 into Witham for approximately 2km

GRANTCHESTER
CAMBRIDGESHIRE

See map p.89 (2)

KEY FIGURES: Rupert Brooke; Virginia Woolf
KEY LOCATIONS: Orchard House; Byron's Pool; The Old Vicarage

While on holiday in Germany before the First World War, Rupert Brooke was gripped by such a strong yearning for Grantchester that he wrote a poem about the village – 'The Sentimental Exile' (better known today as 'The Old Vicarage, Grantchester'). In the poem, Brooke conjures up his world there through such lines as 'Is there honey still for tea?' For Brooke there always was, courtesy of the bees that were kept by Mr Neeve, his landlady's husband.

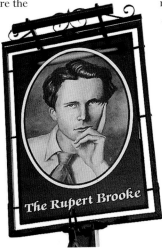

The Rupert Brooke

Brooke first came to the village in 1909, after graduating from King's College, Cambridge. He took rooms at Orchard House, which was also a favourite tearoom with Cambridge students.

Brooke bathed in Byron's Pool, which was named after the poet who once visited it, and entertained his friends, the Grantchester Group, who included E.M. Forster, Bertrand Russell and Virginia Woolf, with picnics on the lawn, long walks and teas. He had first met Virginia when they were children in Cornwall. Virginia also stayed with him at The Old Vicarage, where he moved in 1914. They bathed naked in the moonlight in the Granta. Brooke left Grantchester in 1912 to travel, but the village still maintains strong associations with the poet.

Visitors can still take tea at Orchard House and there is a pub (shown above) named after him.

(i) information

Contact details

Grantchester
Cambridge
Cambridgeshire
CB3 9

Rupert Brooke's Society:
www.rupertbrooke.com
Orchard House:
www.orchard-grantchester.com

Transport links

Cambridge

The M11 passes near
Grantchester

CAMBRIDGE UNIVERSITY

CAMBRIDGE

See map p.89 **3**

KEY FIGURES: M.R. James; E.M. Forster; Samuel Pepys; C.S. Lewis; Charles Kingsley

KEY LOCATIONS: King's College; Magdalene College

Each Christmas Eve, friends would gather in the rooms of M.R. 'Monty' James (1862–1936), the Provost at King's College, Cambridge from 1905, and listen while he read them his ghost stories. The fire crackled, the candles spluttered and the listeners' flesh would creep, for M.R. James was one of the greatest exponents of the classic ghost story. James's 'Oh, Whistle, and I'll Come to You, My Lad', published in *The Collected Ghost Stories of M.R. James* (1931), is regarded as one of the most frightening stories in literature.

Although he is now most famous for such tales, they form only a tiny portion of his literary output – he was also a noted scholar of medieval illuminated manuscripts and apocryphal Biblical literature.

King's College also played a central role in the life of E.M. Forster. He first came to the college in 1897 to read Classics and History. During his first year he had what he disparagingly called a 'puddling' life, but this improved from his second year, as he was given rooms in college and was therefore much more involved in the life of the place. In his fourth year he was elected a member of the Apostles. This was a tremendous accolade because the Apostles formed the intellectual cream of Cambridge, and previous members had included Alfred, Lord Tennyson. In Forster's novel *The Longest Journey* (1907), the opening scene describes a meeting of the Apostles. Forster left Cambridge in June 1901 with a moderately good degree and soon embarked on a year-long journey around Europe, which provided inspiration for what was then his half-formed idea to become a writer.

Forster returned to Cambridge in 1927 on a three-year fellowship, but it was not a wild success. However, he was back again in

THE LION, THE WITCH
and
THE WARDROBE

*A Story for Children
by*
C. S. LEWIS

▲ `C.S. Lewis is probably most famous for his Narnia books, including* The Lion, The Witch and The Wardrobe.

1946 as an Honorary Fellow and was allowed to live at King's College. This was excellent timing because the lease was up on his beloved home, West Hackhurst, and he needed to find somewhere new to live. Forster quickly picked up the threads of life at the university and even joined the Apostles again. He remained a Fellow until just before his death from a stroke in June 1970.

Samuel Pepys spent most of his life amassing his library of more than 3,000 books, and before he died he made provision for them to be left to his old Cambridge college, Magdalene. He studied here in 1651–54, having previously been at Trinity Hall, and returned to the college for nostalgic visits in October 1667 and May 1668. He recorded both events in his famous diary, and noted with pleasure that the beer served in the college buttery was 'the best I ever drank'.

The Pepys' Library is in the Second Court at Magdalene, while the Old Library in the First Court contains manuscripts belonging to three of the college's Honorary Fellows: Thomas Hardy, Rudyard Kipling and T.S. Eliot.

C.S. Lewis (1898–1963) was a Fellow of Magdalen College, Oxford, from 1925 to 1954 and was Professor of Medieval and Renaissance English at Magdalene College, Cambridge, from 1954 to 1963. He wrote several books while working here, including *The Magician's Nephew*, one of his well-loved 'Narnia' tales for children, and *Surprised by Joy*, which were both published in 1955. He died here in 1963 one week before his 65th birthday.

Of course, Magdalene and King's are not the only colleges in Cambridge with literary associations, as generations of writers, poets

▼ *Magdalene College has strong literary associations with such writers as Thomas Hardy, Rudyard Kipling and C.S. Lewis.*

and critics have come here, whether as students, visiting lecturers or college professors.

Among the poets and playwrights who studied here are John Milton (Christ's); Siegfried Sassoon (Clare); Samuel Taylor Coleridge (Jesus); William Wordsworth (St John's); Christopher Marlowe, John Fletcher and John Cowper Powys (Corpus Christi); Rupert Brooke (King's and Trinity); Edmund Spenser (Pembroke); Thomas Gray (Pembroke and Peterhouse); Robert Herrick (St John's and Trinity Hall); and Andrew Marvell, John Dryden, Alfred Tennyson and Lord Byron (Trinity).

Cambridge writers and critics include Hugh Walpole (Emmanuel); Rosamond Lehmann (Girton); Laurence Sterne (Jesus); Horace Walpole, E.F. Benson and Shane Leslie (King's); Charles Kingsley (Magdalene); A.S. Byatt and Margaret Drabble (Newnham); Stephen Fry (Queen's); Malcolm Lowry (St Catharine's); James Frazer, Lytton Strachey and Leonard Woolf (Trinity); and Raphael Holinshed, Leslie Stephen and Ronald Firbank (Trinity Hall).

THE CAMBRIDGE FOOTLIGHTS

When the Cambridge University Footlights Club first opened its doors for one night only in the town theatre (between Emmanuel and the University Arms Hotel), it had 30 members. Some months later the club became known as the 'Footlights'; its aim was to provide entertainment for the general public and it was to perform every week in May at the Theatre Royal. Although its performers drew on Victorian farces, one-act plays and burlesques for their material, from 1892 onwards they produced only original material. From 1919 to 1939, the club rented rooms in the Masonic Hall, Corn Exchange Street. In 1936, after the Cambridge Arts Theatre opened, the club put on the first of 53 May Week Revues there. Today, the club has no official home. It has since put on thousands of shows, not just in Cambridge but in London and Edinburgh, among other places. It was also the early stamping ground of many talented writers and comedians, including John Cleese, Peter Cook, Clive James, Stephen Fry, Emma Thompson and Hugh Laurie.

ⓘ information

Contact details

Cambridge University
Cambridge

☎ +44 (0)871 226 8006

🖥 Tourist Information for Cambridge:
www.visitcambridge.org

Transport links

🚆 Cambridge

🚗 The M11 and A14 go through Cambridge

NEWMARKET HEATH

SUFFOLK

See map p.89 (4)

KEY FIGURES: Dick Francis; Bob Champion; John Francome
KEY LOCATION: Newmarket Heath

For some reason, East Anglia has long attracted writers of detective and crime fiction: Dorothy L. Sayers, Margery Allingham, P.D. James (born 1920) and Ruth Rendell (born 1930) have all had strong associations with the area. Dick Francis (1920–2010) is another noted author who had associations with the region. Francis wrote more than 30 thrillers, most of which revolve around the sport of horse racing and some of which are set in the Suffolk market town of Newmarket.

Dick Francis was such an expert on horse racing because he used to be a champion National Hunt jockey and rode horses owned by the late Queen Mother from 1953 to 1957. He suffered a couple of serious falls and gave up racing and turned his hand to writing. After writing his autobiography, *The Sport of Queens* (1957), he worked as racing correspondent for a newspaper for 16 years, before branching out into crime fiction. His first novel, *Dead Cert* (shown right), was published in 1962. Other jockeys have followed in his literary footsteps, including Bob Champion and John Francome.

Francis moved to Florida with his wife, Mary, in the 1980s and he died at his home in Grand Cayman in 2010.

dead cert

Dick Francis

(i) information

Contact details

Newmarket
Suffolk

🖥 Tourist Information:
www.newmarket.org.uk

Transport links

🚆 Newmarket

🚗 The A14 goes through
Newmarket

ALDEBURGH

SUFFOLK

See map p.89 ⑤

KEY FIGURES:	Benjamin Britten; George Crabbe; Wilkie Collins; M.R. James
KEY LOCATION:	Aldeburgh Church

A chain of literary events led the composer, Benjamin Britten (1913–76), to set up the Aldeburgh Music Festival in 1948. He had read an article by E.M. Forster about the 18th-century poet, George Crabbe (1754–1832), who had a strong love of the sea and of the coastal town of Aldeburgh, where he was born. Britten could understand Crabbe's affection for the Suffolk coastline, as he had grown up in Lowestoft, a few miles to the north of Aldeburgh. After reading Crabbe's poem *The Borough* (1810), Britten was inspired to write the opera *Peter Grimes* (1945). It was based on a character from Crabbe's poem, a fisherman overcome with remorse at the way he had treated his apprentices. In 1947, a bust of the poet was erected in the local church.

In 1951, E.M. Forster once again played an important part in Britten's life when he and Eric Crozier wrote the libretto for another Britten opera, *Billy Budd*, which was based on a story by Herman Melville (1819–91).

Britten, Crabbe and Forster are not the only famous names associated with Aldeburgh. Wilkie Collins visited the town in 1862 and gave his novel *No Name* (1862) a local setting. He had already written his mystery novel, *The Woman in White* (1860), and followed it with *The Moonstone* in 1868, which is widely claimed to be the first British detective novel.

Aldeburgh also appealed to M.R. James, whose ghost stories can still send shivers up the spine of anyone brave enough to read them while sitting alone in a room. As a child, James visited his grandfather here, and towards the end of his life he liked to holiday in Aldeburgh each year.

ⓘ information

Contact details
Aldeburgh
Suffolk

🌐 Local Information:
www.aldeburgh-uk.com

Transport links
🚉 Melton

🚗 The A12 passes near Aldeburgh

DUNWICH
SUFFOLK

See map p.89 **6**

KEY FIGURES: Edward Fitzgerald; Thomas Carlyle; P.D. James
KEY LOCATION: Dunwich

In 1855, Edward Fitzgerald (1809–83) brought his great friend, Thomas Carlyle, to the village of Dunwich, on the Suffolk coast. Fitzgerald returned in 1859 while he was translating *The Rubáiyát of Omar Khayyám* from the Persian. The first translation was published anonymously, but Fitzgerald put his name to the three later revised editions of the poem. Although he wrote other books, he is best remembered for this work.

Fitzgerald and Carlyle were not the only literary figures to come here, as Henry James, Algernon Swinburne (who was inspired by the village to write 'By the North Sea') and Jerome K. Jerome (1859–1927), the author of *Three Men in a Boat* (1889), all visited this beautiful stretch of Suffolk's coast.

In 1911, the author of *Anne of Green Gables* (1908), Lucy Maud Montgomery (1874–1942), visited Dunwich during her honeymoon.

The crime writer P.D. James has also been inspired by Dunwich and the surrounding area. The wide, often desolate, beaches of Suffolk are the backdrop to many of her novels and some of them are set around Dunwich.

ⓘ information

Contact details

Dunwich Heath: Coastal
Centre and Beach
Dunwich, Saxmundham
Suffolk IP17 3DJ

+44 (0)1728 648501

National Trust
(Dunwich Heath):
www.nationaltrust.org.uk

Transport links

Darsham

The A12 passes near
Dunwich

The Dunwich coast features in P. D. James's Unnatural Causes *(1967), which opens with a corpse in a boat.*

CENTRAL ENGLAND

Here is a region full of contrasts, from the golden stones of pretty Cotswold villages to the black slag heaps that were produced by Nottingham's coal-mining industry. Laurie Lee charmed millions of readers when he wrote of his idyllic childhood in the tiny village of Slad, while D.H. Lawrence conjured up a harsh picture of grime and death, which were always waiting just round the corner, when writing of his native Nottinghamshire. John Bunyan was imprisoned for his religious beliefs in Bedford gaol, which inspired him to write *The Pilgrim's Progress*. Lord Byron had a very different moral code, which he indulged while living in his ancestral home of Newstead Abbey. Some of England's greatest educational establishments are in this part of England, including Eton College, Rugby School and Oxford's dreaming spires, which have inspired writers from Thomas Hardy to Colin Dexter.

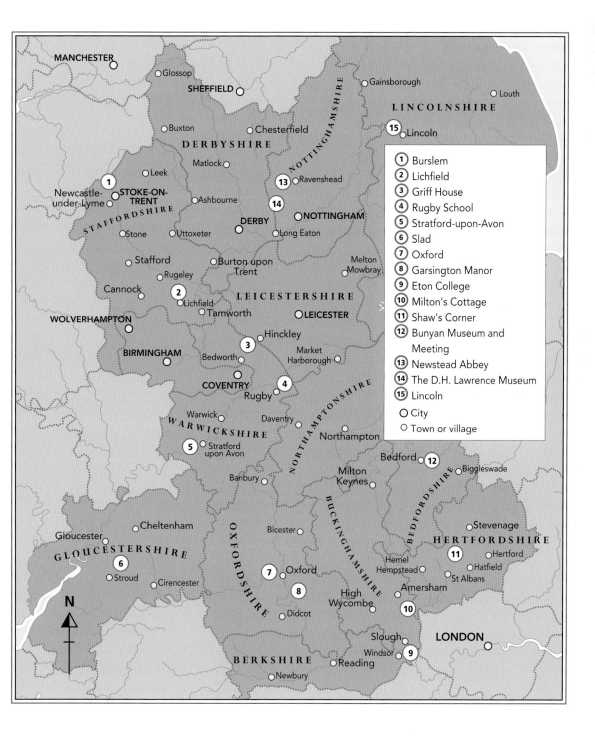

MANCHESTER

Glossop

SHEFFIELD

Gainsborough

Louth

LINCOLNSHIRE

Buxton

Chesterfield

15 Lincoln

D E R B Y S H I R E

Matlock

NOTTINGHAMSHIRE

Leek

1 STOKE-ON-TRENT

Newcastle-under-Lyme

13 Ravenshead

Ashbourne

14

S T A F F O R D S H I R E

Stone

Uttoxeter

DERBY

NOTTINGHAM

Long Eaton

Stafford

Burton upon Trent

Melton Mowbray

Rugeley

Cannock

2

L E I C E S T E R S H I R E

Lichfield

Tamworth

LEICESTER

WOLVERHAMPTON

Hinckley

BIRMINGHAM

3

Bedworth

Market Harborough

COVENTRY

4

Rugby

N O R T H A M P T O N S H I R E

Warwick

Daventry

W A R W I C K S H I R E

Northampton

5 Stratford upon Avon

Bedford

12

Biggleswade

B E D F O R D S H I R E

Banbury

Milton Keynes

B U C K I N G H A M S H I R E

Stevenage

H E R T F O R D S H I R E

Cheltenham

Bicester

11

Hertford

Gloucester

O X F O R D S H I R E

Hemel Hempstead

Hatfield

G L O U C E S T E R S H I R E

6

7 Oxford

St Albans

Amersham

Stroud

Cirencester

8

High Wycombe

10

N

Didcot

Slough

LONDON

Windsor

9

B E R K S H I R E

Reading

Newbury

1	Burslem
2	Lichfield
3	Griff House
4	Rugby School
5	Stratford-upon-Avon
6	Slad
7	Oxford
8	Garsington Manor
9	Eton College
10	Milton's Cottage
11	Shaw's Corner
12	Bunyan Museum and Meeting
13	Newstead Abbey
14	The D.H. Lawrence Museum
15	Lincoln
O	City
O	Town or village

BURSLEM
STAFFORDSHIRE

See map p.89 **1**

KEY FIGURE: Arnold Bennett
KEY LOCATIONS: Burslem Park; Burslem Cemetery

This is one of the 'Five Towns' that feature in the novels by Arnold Bennett (shown right) set in and around the Staffordshire Potteries. However, Bennett renamed them all, so Burslem became Bursley; Hanley (where he was born in 1867) became Hanbridge; Tunstall was transformed into Turnhill; Longton turned into Longshaw; and Stoke-on-Trent became Knype. Bennett's Five Towns, together with Fenton, were united in the borough of Stoke-on-Trent in 1910.

Bennett wrote 13 novels and three collections of short stories about the places where he grew up and the effect that the pottery industry had on the people who lived there. However, his novels were written from memory as he left Staffordshire for London when he was 21, and moved to Paris for ten years in 1902. His first novel, *A Man from the North*, was published in 1898, but Bennett really started to make a name for himself with *Anna of the Five Towns* (1902), which tells the story of a miser's daughter. *The Old Wives' Tale* (1908) was particularly successful and drew on many of his childhood memories. By now Bennett was starting to earn serious money, and he eventually became one of the highest paid writers of his day.

Many of the places in the Five Towns appear in Bennett's novels and stories, and in Burslem some of them are marked by plaques. Burslem Park is mentioned in *Anna of the Five Towns* and in *Clayhanger* (1910). After Bennett died in 1931, his ashes were buried in the cemetery at Burslem.

ⓘ information

Contact details
Burslem
Stoke-on-Trent
Staffordshire
ST6

Transport links
🚆 Longport

🚗 The A53 and the A50 pass near to Burslem

LICHFIELD
STAFFORDSHIRE

See map p.89 ②

KEY FIGURE: Dr Samuel Johnson
KEY LOCATIONS: Breadmarket Street; Market Street; St Mary's Church; Dam Street

Dr Samuel Johnson (shown below) was born in 1709 over his father's bookshop in Breadmarket Street, Lichfield. This was an apt location for one who grew up to become a writer, critic and the compiler of the first English dictionary. His birthplace is now a museum devoted to his memory. A statue of him stands in Market Street. Johnson was baptized in St Mary's Church and took his first lessons at the age of five at Dame Oliver's School in Dam Street. Later, he attended the local grammar school, which originally stood in St John's Street before being moved to Borrowcrop Hill in 1903. In 1728, Johnson went to Pembroke College, Oxford (see pages 106–7), but he could not afford to stay and left just over a year later without his degree. In 1735 he married Mrs Elizabeth Porter and the couple opened a private school in Edial, near Lichfield. The school wasn't as financially successful as the couple had anticipated, so in 1737 Johnson left for London with one of his pupils, David Garrick (1717–79).

There are memorials to both Johnson and Garrick in Lichfield Cathedral. There is also a memorial to the poet Anna Seward (1747–1809), who lived at the Bishop's Palace (her father was the canon of the cathedral) from 1754 to 1809.

Nathaniel Hawthorne (1804–64) was another literary pilgrim who was keen to trace Johnson's life in Lichfield, and he wrote of his visit in *Our Old Home* (1863).

ⓘ information

Contact details
Lichfield
Staffordshire, WS13

+44 (0)1543 412112

🖳 Tourist Information:
www.visitlichfield.co.uk

Transport links
🚆 Lichfield City

🚗 The A51 and the A38
pass through Lichfield

GRIFF HOUSE
WARWICKSHIRE

See map p.89 ③

KEY FIGURE: George Eliot
KEY LOCATIONS: Griff House; Chilvers Coton; Arbury Hall

The novelist George Eliot (shown right) looked back on her childhood at Griff House (now a hotel) with great affection. She was born Mary Anne Evans in 1819 and her family moved to Griff House when she was five months old. The house included a farmyard and pool, and it is easy to detect the character of her childhood home in the opening chapters of *The Mill on the Floss* (1860).

There were many pools, water pumps and canals around Griff House, and this proximity to water certainly influenced Eliot's career as a novelist – water is a recurrent theme in *The Mill on the Floss*. She lived here until the spring of 1841 when she and her father moved to Foleshill in Coventry. Her brother, Isaac, and his new wife, Sarah, moved into Griff House, where they stayed for the rest of their lives.

The area around Griff House was the inspiration for many places in her novels.

She based Shepperton Church in *Scenes of Clerical Life* (1858) on the church at Chilvers Coton; and Arbury Hall, which was the 'the big house' on the estate that her father managed when she was a child, became Cheverel Manor in the same book.

ⓘ information

Contact details

Griff House Beefeater and
  Premier Inn
Coventry Road
Nuneaton
Warwickshire, CV10 7PJ

🖥 Local Information (Griff House):
www.visitnorthernwarwickshire.
com

Transport links

🚃 Nuneaton

🚌 The A444 passes through
  Nuneaton

RUGBY SCHOOL
WARWICKSHIRE

See map p.89 (4)

KEY FIGURES: Thomas Hughes; Dr Thomas Arnold
KEY LOCATION: Rugby School

The title page of *Tom Brown's Schooldays* (1857) announces that it was written by 'An Old Boy'. This old boy was Thomas Hughes, who attended Rugby School (shown below) from 1834 to 1842. His novel praises the then headmaster, Dr Thomas Arnold (1795–1842), who built the foundations of the public school system in Britain. Taking inspiration from his time at Rugby, Hughes championed what became known as 'muscular Christianity', which combined a strong Christian belief with prowess on the sports field, loyalty to one's school and country, and courage. Many other old boys similarly inspired include Dr Arnold's son Matthew (1822–88), who became the poet, critic and champion of secondary education; A.P. Stanley (1815–81), who wrote *The Life and Correspondence of Thomas Arnold* (1844); and the poet Arthur Clough (1819–61).

(i) information

Contact details

Rugby School
Rugby
Warwickshire CV22 5EH

☎ +44 (0)1788 556216

Rugby School:
www.rugbyschool.net

Transport links

Rugby

The A426 passes through Rugby

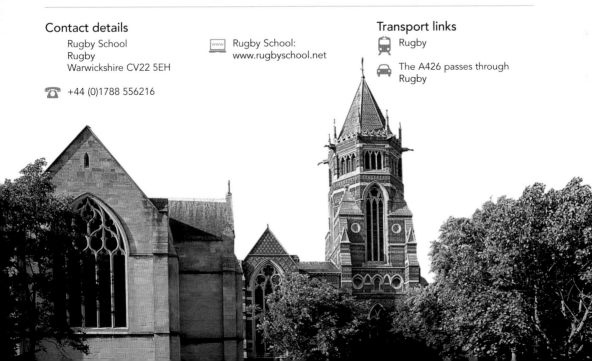

STRATFORD-UPON-AVON

WARWICKSHIRE

See map p.89 (5)

KEY FIGURES: William Shakespeare; Washington Irving; Marie Corelli
KEY LOCATIONS: Henley Street; Hall's Croft; Holy Trinity Church; Bridge Street

Shakespeare and Stratford. The words go together like Romeo and Juliet. Stratford is the old market town where William Shakespeare (1564–1616) was born, educated and married, and where he later lived. Born in a half-timbered house in Henley Street, Shakespeare's exact date of birth is disputed, although it is generally believed to be 23 April. The bedroom in which Shakespeare is thought to have been born is not only interesting in its own right, but has the added attraction of some literary graffiti on the window where such luminaries as Sir Walter Scott, Isaac Watts and Thomas Carlyle scratched their names.

Only the foundations and the garden remain from Shakespeare's last home, New Place. However, Hall's Croft, the home of his daughter Susanna and her husband, Dr John Hall, is well worth visiting. Mary Arden's House, which was the home of Shakespeare's mother, is at Wilmcote, just outside Stratford, and Anne Hathaway's Cottage at Shottery was the family home of Shakespeare's wife. When Shakespeare died in 1616 he was buried in the chancel of Holy Trinity Church.

Other literary luminaries visited Stratford. Washington Irving (1783–1859), the satirist and poet, stayed at the Red Horse in Bridge Street in 1818, under the assumed name of Geoffrey Crayon, and wrote about his visit in *The Sketch-Book of Geoffrey Crayon, Gent.* (1819–20). Marie Corelli (1855–1924), who wrote romantic melodramas, moved to Stratford in 1901. She is believed to be the inspiration for E.F. Benson's larger-than-life character Lucia.

Mrs Gaskell first ventured into print when she wrote about Stratford in William Howitt's *Visits to Remarkable Places* (1840). She knew the town, having attended Avonbank School there.

(i) information

Contact details

Stratford-upon-Avon
Warwickshire
CV37

[www] Tourist Information:
www.stratford-upon-avon.
co.uk

Transport links

Stratford-upon-Avon

The A439 and the A422 pass through Stratford-upon-Avon

SLAD
GLOUCESTERSHIRE

See map p.89 **6**

KEY FIGURE:	Laurie Lee
KEY LOCATION:	The Woolpack Inn

Laurie Lee's lyrical account of growing up in Slad, *Cider with Rosie* (1959), describes a lost world. It tells of the English countryside between the two World Wars, abundant with flowers and sweet grass, where large families were crammed into a few rooms, and choirboys trekked through the snow each Christmas to earn money from carol-singing. There were the two grannies who lived next door to each other in a permanent state of war and, of course, Rosie who introduced the young Laurie to the delights of cider.

Laurie Lee (1914–97) arrived in Slad in 1917 when he was three, and 'there with a sense of bewilderment and terror my life in the village began'. He was frightened by the grass, which he had only ever seen at a distance until that moment and which towered over him. He left for London when he was 19, and then went to Spain on a journey that he describes in the second

▲ *Slad was Laurie Lee's childhood home, and his autobiographies capture its charms and problems.*

book of his autobiographical trilogy, *As I Walked Out One Midsummer Morning* (1969). Lee returned to Slad in the 1960s with his wife, Cathy, and he stayed here until his death. He lived near his local pub, the Woolpack Inn. The final part of the trilogy, *A Monument of War*, was published in 1991.

(i) information

Contact details
Slad
Stroud
Gloucestershire
GL6

Transport links
 Stroud

 The A46 passes by Slad and the B4070 passes through

OXFORD
OXFORDSHIRE

See map p.89 (7)

KEY FIGURES: Thomas Hardy; Lewis Carroll; W. H. Auden; William Morris; J.R.R. Tolkien; C.S. Lewis; Sir John Betjeman; Cecil Day-Lewis

KEY LOCATIONS: Various colleges of Oxford University; Jericho

From Dorothy L. Sayers to Colin Dexter (born 1930), Percy Bysshe Shelley to Philip Larkin (1922–85), Lewis Carroll to Philip Pullman (born 1946), Oxford fairly bristles with literary connections.

Thomas Hardy turned Oxford into Christminster in *Jude the Obscure* (1895), in which the eponymous character lodged in the Jericho area of the city. Evelyn Waugh (1903–66) was an undergraduate at Hertford College and transformed his experiences into a nostalgic, golden idyll in *Brideshead Revisited* (1945). The novel combined snobbery and Roman Catholicism, which were two of Waugh's guiding principles.

Dorothy L. Sayers drew on her time as an undergraduate at Somerville for her detective novel, *Gaudy Night* (1935), in which Harriet Vane solves a mystery at her old college while being romanced by Lord Peter Wimsey, a character who also knew Oxford well, having been created a Balliol man. More recently, devotees of Colin Dexter, who lives in the city, have developed a useful knowledge of Oxford through his detective novels, which feature

▲ Lewis Carroll's Mad Hatter is thought to be based on eccentric Oxford inventor Theophilus Carter.

the irascible Inspector Morse and his trusty sergeant, Lewis.

Charles Dodgson became Master and tutor at Christ Church in 1855, and taught here for the rest of his life. The world knows him better as Lewis Carroll, who immortalized his young friend, Alice Liddell, in *Alice's Adventures in Wonderland* (1865) and *Through the Looking Glass and What Alice Found There* (1871). Other writers

Philip Pullman's trilogy of children's books are set partly in the Oxford we know but also in an alternative and fantastical Oxford.

who went to Christ Church include the Elizabethan poet Sir Philip Sidney (1554–86), John Ruskin and W.H. Auden (1907–73), who was later Professor of Poetry.

William Morris was at Exeter College from 1853 to 1855, and 40 years later his writings enthralled a young Exeter undergraduate called J.R.R. Tolkien (1892–1973). He spent over 30 years as a Professor at Exeter, during which period he also created his own world of Middle Earth in *The Hobbit* (1937) and *The Lord of the Rings* (1954–55). Tolkien was a colleague of C.S. Lewis, who was a Fellow at Magdalen College from 1925 to 1954. While he was at Oxford, Lewis wrote many books including *The Screwtape Letters* (1942) and began the Narnia stories.

Sir John Betjeman studied with Lewis at Magdalen College. He described his time at Oxford in his verse-autobiography *Summoned by Bells* (1960). While he was here he became friends with a group of poets that included Auden and Louis MacNeice (1907–63), who went to Merton College. He also mixed with Stephen Spender (1909–95), who was at University College, and Cecil Day-Lewis, who was at Wadham College. Day-Lewis and Auden edited *Oxford Poetry* in 1927, and in the 1950s Day-Lewis became Professor of Poetry here. He wrote about his Oxford life in *The Buried Day* (1960).

To young readers, Oxford is synonymous with Philip Pullman's trilogy of books *The Northern Lights*, *The Subtle Knife* and *The Amber Spyglass*.

(i) information

Contact details

Oxford
Oxfordshire

☎ +44 (0)1865 252200

 Tourist Information:
www.visitoxfordandoxfordshire.com

Transport links

🚆 Oxford

🚗 The A40 and the A34 pass through Oxford

GARSINGTON MANOR

OXFORDSHIRE

See map p.89 (8)

KEY FIGURES: Philip and Lady Ottoline Morrell; Aldous Huxley; D.H. Lawrence
KEY LOCATION: Garsington Manor

Between 1915 and 1928, Garsington Manor (shown right) was the home of Philip and Lady Ottoline Morrell, who were members of the Bloomsbury Group. Lady Ottoline loved filling her Elizabethan manor house with the cream of the youthful literary set; her guests included such luminaries as Lytton Strachey; Siegfried Sassoon; D.H. Lawrence; T.S. Eliot; Katherine Mansfield; Bertrand Russell (with whom Lady Ottoline had a long-running affair); and Aldous Huxley.

Lady Ottoline, with her long, horse-like face and strange clothes, was an irresistible target for writers of the period and for those who came later. Huxley was the first to take inspiration from her eccentric character in his novel, *Crome Yellow* (1921). Crome, the house in the novel, was obviously based on Garsington, and the main characters, Henry and 'Old Priscilla' Wimbush were undoubtedly Philip and Ottoline. D.H. Lawrence turned her into Hermione Roddice

in *Women in Love* and she was the inspiration for Lady Sybilline Quarrell mentioned in *Forty Years On* (1968), a play by Alan Bennett (born 1934).

(i) information

Contact details

Garsington Manor
Garsington
Oxfordshire, OX44 9DH

Tourist Information:
www.visitoxfordandoxfordshire.com

Transport links

Radley

The B480 passes by Garsington

ETON COLLEGE
BERKSHIRE

See map p.89 (9)

KEY FIGURES: Percy Bysshe Shelley; Ian Fleming; Cyril Connolly; Aldous Huxley
KEY LOCATION: Eton College

This is probably the most famous school in Britain, if not the world. It has the distinction of having been founded by Henry VI (1422–71) in 1440, and later enjoyed the patronage of George III (1760–1820). The list of distinguished Old Etonians is endless and even includes the fictional character of James Bond. This is hardly surprising as his creator, Ian Fleming, was an Old Etonian, as was his brother, Peter.

Percy Bysshe Shelley (1792–1822) came to Eton in 1804 where he wrote the Gothic novel *Zastrozzi* (1810). Other Old Etonian poets include Thomas Gray; Algernon Swinburne; Robert Bridges; Sir Osbert and Sir Sacheverell Sitwell; and Hugo Williams. Many other writers are Old Etonians, including Henry Fielding; Horace Walpole; Anthony Powell; George Orwell; Cyril Connolly, who wrote about his schooldays in *Enemies of Promise* (1938); Robin Maugham;

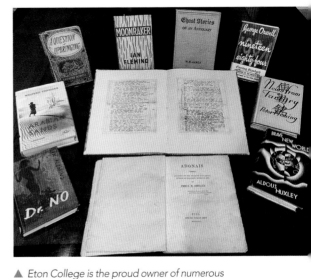

▲ *Eton College is the proud owner of numerous first editions by its literary alumni.*

Nicholas Mosley; Aldous Huxley, who also taught here from 1917 to 1919; M.R. James (who became Provost in 1918); John Lehmann; James Lees-Milne; Nigel Nicolson; and Henry Green.

(i) information

Contact details

Eton College
Windsor
Berkshire, SL4 6DW

 +44 (0)1753 671000

Eton College:
www.etoncollege.com

Transport links

Windsor and Eton Central
Windsor and Eton Riverside

The M4 passes through
Windsor

MILTON'S COTTAGE
BUCKINGHAMSHIRE

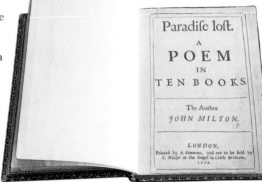

See map p.89 (10)

KEY FIGURE: John Milton
KEY LOCATION: Milton's Cottage Museum

Although this is called 'Milton's Cottage', the great poet only spent a short time here from 1665 to 1666. Its importance comes from being the only home of the poet's to have survived.

John Milton (1608–74) brought his family to Chalfont St Giles from London in 1665 to escape the Great Plague. The move to the countryside was orchestrated by Thomas Ellwood, who was a pupil of Milton's.

Despite Milton's difficult marriage to Elizabeth Minshull, and his blindness, he managed to put the finishing touches to *Paradise Lost* (1667) while at the cottage. An early edition can be found on display at the cottage today (shown left). It was a return to poetry after having spent some time writing political pamphlets.

The cottage garden at Milton's Cottage is planted with many of the flowers that Milton mentions in his poetry. Completely blind, as he had been since 1651, Milton could only smell the flowers that grew here. It seems fitting that he composed his epic poem about the fall of Adam and Eve from

(i) information

Contact details

Milton's Cottage Museum
21 Deanway
Chalfont St Giles
Buckinghamshire
HP8 4JH

www Milton Cottage Trust
www.miltonscottage.org

☎ +44 (0)1494 872313

Transport links

🚉 Chalfont and Latimer
Gerrards Cross

🚗 The A413 passes by
Chalfont St Giles

SHAW'S CORNER
HERTFORDSHIRE

See map p.89 (11)

KEY FIGURE: George Bernard Shaw
KEY LOCATION: Shaw's Corner

In 1904 playwright George Bernard Shaw (1856–1950) and his wife, Charlotte, moved into the house that the villagers would refer to as 'Shaw's Corner'. Neither particularly liked it at the time, yet it was the place where they were to remain for the rest of their lives. At first they rented the house, finally buying it 14 years later.

Initially, the villagers of Ayot St Lawrence were unsure of Shaw. Their suspicions increased after the publication of his anti-war pamphlet *Common Sense about the War* (1914), which led to threats of violence against him. Shaw was finally accepted by the village in 1915 when he helped to clear up after the great Hertfordshire Blizzard, which laid waste to the surrounding countryside.

Charlotte died in September 1943, and Shaw was grief-stricken. He died in November 1950, leaving the house to the National Trust.

▲ *Shaw wrote in a hut-cum-summerhouse, which had a revolving base so he could follow the sun.*

ⓘ information

Contact details

Shaw's Corner
Ayot St Lawrence
Welwyn
Hertfordshire, AL6 9BX

www National Trust:
www.nationaltrust.org.uk/main/
w-shawscorner

☎ +44 (0)1438 829221

Transport links

🚆 Welwyn North

🚗 The A1(M) passes near Ayot St Lawrence

BUNYAN MUSEUM AND MEETING

BEDFORDSHIRE

See map p.89 **12**

KEY FIGURE: John Bunyan
KEY LOCATION: Bedford

John Bunyan (1628–88), who is most famous as the author of *The Pilgrim's Progress* (1684), was a minister in Bedford from late 1671 until his death. He first became a preacher in 1653, but fell foul of the powers-that-be in November 1660 for preaching without a licence and spent most of the next 12 years in Bedford Gaol. The site of his former imprisonment is marked at the point where Silver Street and the High Street meet. Nearby, at the corner of St Peter's Street and the Broadway, is Sir Joseph Boehm's bronze statue of Bunyan with his Bible in his left hand.

Bunyan did not allow imprisonment to slow him down, and he wrote nine books during his stay in Bedford Gaol, including *Grace Abounding to the Chief of Sinners* (1666), which tells the story of his life and how he found God. Bunyan was released from prison in 1672, but was briefly incarcerated again in 1676, during which period he once again put pen to paper. This time, the result was the first part of *The Pilgrim's Progress*, which was published in 1674; he completed it in 1684. Many of the places mentioned in the book are modelled on those in and around Bedford, such as Stevington Cross where Christian dropped his burden.

The original barn where Bunyan preached has long since vanished and been replaced by the Bunyan Museum, which contains some of Bunyan's belongings as well as copies of his books.

(i) information

Contact details

Bunyan Meeting
Mill Street
Bedford
Bedfordshire, MK40 3EU

☎ +44 (0)1234 213722

Bunyan Meeting :
www.bunyanmeeting.co.uk

Transport links

Bedford St Johns
Bedford

The A6 passes through
Bedford

NEWSTEAD ABBEY
NOTTINGHAMSHIRE

See map p.89 **13**

KEY FIGURES: George Gordon, Lord Byron
KEY LOCATIONS: Newstead Abbey; Hucknall Torkard Church

---

eorge Gordon, Lord Byron (1788–1824; shown right) was the great literary celebrity of his day. He was a baron and he owned Newstead Abbey, a 12th-century estate that had been in the family since 1540. Byron was wildly handsome and he was a celebrated poet, having received critical acclaim for the first two cantos of *Childe Harold's Pilgrimage* (1812). Byron also liked to throw parties. Those he hosted at Newstead Abbey raised the eyebrows of the local worthies, especially when they heard that one of the drinking vessels was a skull-goblet.

By the time Byron was 24, in 1812, he had travelled widely and scored a notable success with *Childe Harold*. That same year he met his future wife, Annabella Milbanke, and started affairs with three other women. Byron married Annabella in January 1815 and their daughter, Ada, was born that December. However, the marriage was over by January 1816. The scandal surrounding this parting, coupled with Byron's financial difficulties, forced him to leave England in April 1816. Thomas Wildman, an old school friend of Byron, bought Newstead Abbey from him in 1818 for £94,500.

By late 1823 Byron was in Greece, where he died in April 1824. His body was returned to England and buried in the Byron family vault at Hucknall Torkard Church, near Newstead Abbey.

Newstead Abbey is open to the public and one of the most popular sights is the grave of Byron's favourite dog, Boatswain, who died in 1808.

(i) information

Contact details

Newstead Abbey Historic
House and Gardens
Newstead Abbey Park
Nottingham, NG15 8NA

Newstead Abbey:
www.newsteadabbey.org.uk

Transport links

Newstead

The A60 passes near
to Newstead Abbey

☏ +44 (0)1623 455900

D. H. LAWRENCE MUSEUM

NOTTINGHAMSHIRE

See map p.89 **14**

KEY FIGURE: D.H. Lawrence
KEY LOCATION: D.H. Lawrence Museum

David Herbert Lawrence (shown right) was born here on 11 September 1885. He was the fourth child of an illiterate father and an educated mother. This mismatch between his parents caused immense friction within the family because his mother wanted her son to escape the almost inevitable working-class fate of working down the mines.

Once he had moved away from Nottingham, Lawrence described it as 'the country of my heart', but this was a classic case of distance lending enchantment to the view because he disliked it when he lived here. For one thing, the smoky air did nothing for his weak lungs and he twice became ill with pneumonia.

Lawrence won a scholarship to Nottingham High School, which he attended from 1898 to 1901, and then left at the age of 16 to work as a clerk in a Nottingham factory. This phase ended after he developed pneumonia and it was while he was convalescing that he met Jessie Chambers, who urged him to write. His first short story was published in the local paper in 1907, while he was training to be a teacher at University College, Nottingham.

After another bout of pneumonia in 1911, Lawrence decided to abandon teaching for full-time writing. In the same year he fell in love with Frieda Weekley, the German wife of his old professor at Nottingham. She left her family in 1912 and ran away with Lawrence, first to Germany and then to Italy. Lawrence married Frieda in London in July 1914, 'with neuralgia in my left eye and my heart in my boots'.

ⓘ information

Contact details

D.H. Lawrence Birthplace Museum
8a Victoria Street
Eastwood
Nottinghamshire, NG16 3AW

[www] Broxtow Borough Council:
www.broxtowe.gov.uk

Transport links

Langley Mill

 The A608 passes through Eastwood and the A610 passes by

LINCOLN
LINCOLNSHIRE

See map p.89 (15)

KEY FIGURE: Alfred, Lord Tennyson
KEY LOCATIONS: Lincoln Cathedral; Usher Gallery; Lincoln Central Library

Just as Lincoln Cathedral dominates the area for miles around, so the statue of Alfred, Lord Tennyson (shown right) by George Frederick Watts (1817–1904) dominates the city's Cathedral Close. Tennyson was a son of the county and retained strong links with it, so deserved such grand commemoration. Many artefacts connected with Tennyson are held in the Tennyson Room in Lincoln's Usher Gallery and in the Tennyson Research Centre in Lincoln Central Library.

Tennyson was born in Somersby in Lincolnshire in August 1809, to the Reverend George Clayton Tennyson and his wife, Elizabeth. The young Tennyson was strongly influenced by the poetry of George Gordon, Lord Byron, and was devastated when he died in 1824. In 1833, Tennyson was once again consumed with grief when his dearest friend, Arthur Hallam, died. He began to write *In Memoriam*, a long elegy for his friend, which was not published until 1850, the year after he became Poet Laureate. The statue was erected after his death in 1892.

(i) information

Contact details

Lincoln
Lincolnshire

 Tourist Information:
www.visitlincolnshire.com

Transport links

Lincoln Central

The A46, the A57 and the A15 pass through Lincoln

NORTHERN ENGLAND

Stretching from Yorkshire up to Cumbria and Northumberland, this area has some of the most spectacular scenery in England. It is hardly surprising, therefore, that for centuries it has attracted writers and poets who are inspired by the landscape, from Bram Stoker whose Gothic imagination was fired by an incident during a visit to Whitby in North Yorkshire, to the Romantic poets who flocked to the Lake District in a movement that was headed by William Wordsworth and Samuel Taylor Coleridge. Agatha Christie became embroiled in a mystery that could have been taken straight out of one of her detective books in Harrogate, while the dramatic countryside around Haworth and a difficult home life prompted a creative outpouring from Charlotte, Anne and Emily Brontë.

①	Wordsworth's Cumbria
②	Beatrix Potter's Cumbria
③	Lake Windemere and Coniston Water
④	Liverpool
⑤	Manchester
⑥	Brontë Parsonage Museum
⑦	The Old Swan Hotel
⑧	Shandy Hall
⑨	Scarborough
⑩	Whitby
⑪	Durham Cathedral
⑫	The Morden Tower
○	City
○	Town or village

NORTHUMBERLAND

Morpeth
Blyth

TYNE & WEAR
⑫ NEWCASTLE UPON TYNE
Consett SUNDERLAND

Carlisle

CUMBRIA

DURHAM
Durham ⑪

①

Penrith

Stockton-on-Tees
Middlesbrough
Appleby-in-Westmorland
Darlington

Lake District

⑩ Whitby

②
③ Kendal

North York Moors

Northallerton

Scarborough
⑨

Ulverston

NORTH YORKSHIRE

Hawes

⑧

Ripon

Morecambe Lancaster

EAST RIDING OF YORKSHIRE

Harrogate ⑦ York Tadcaster

Beverley

LANCASHIRE

⑥ Keighley

Blackpool

Preston

BRADFORD LEEDS
Halifax

HULL

Blackburn

Huddersfield

Southport

Bolton

Crosby Kirkby

Doncaster

LIVERPOOL
Birkenhead ④ Warrington

⑤ MANCHESTER
Stockport

SHEFFIELD

N

WORDSWORTH'S CUMBRIA

CUMBRIA

See map p. 117 ①

KEY FIGURES: William Wordsworth; Samuel Taylor Coleridge; Thomas De Quincey
KEY LOCATIONS: Wordsworth House; Dove Cottage; Allan Bank; Rydal Mount

William Wordsworth's (1770–1850) love of Cumbria began in his childhood. He spent most of his life there, and longed for the countryside whenever he was travelling. Three houses are associated with his life in Cumbria.

Wordsworth House

In his poem *The Prelude* (1850), Wordsworth described many of his childhood memories, including the delight he took in the River Derwent. It ran past the foot of Wordsworth House, which the Wordsworth family rented from Sir James Lowther, the local landowner who employed John Wordsworth, William's father, as his land agent. William Wordsworth was born here on 7 April 1770, and his devoted sister, Dorothy (1771–1855), on Christmas Day 1771.

Wordsworth developed his love of literature from spending hours in the library at Wordsworth House. It was a happy childhood until 1778 when Wordsworth's mother, Ann, died. Dorothy was sent to stay with relatives in Halifax and did not see William again for nine years. Wordsworth House ceased to be the family home when John died at the end of 1782. It was not the end of Wordsworth's life in the Lake District, however.

Dove Cottage

William and Dorothy moved into Dove Cottage on 20 December 1799. Dove Cottage was all the Wordsworths could afford – it was small and simple, with stone walls and a roof of local slate.

Dorothy's Journal, which Dorothy kept between 1800 and 1803, is a vivid description of life at Dove Cottage and served as inspiration for many of her brother's poems, including 'Home at Grasmere'. In October 1802, William brought his bride, Mary Hutchinson, to live at Dove Cottage. Children soon followed, and their three eldest, John, Dora and Thomas, were all born in the downstairs bedroom at Dove Cottage.

Wordsworth's great friend, Samuel Taylor Coleridge (1772–1834), moved to Keswick with his family in 1800 and was a frequent visitor to Dove Cottage. However, Coleridge's addiction to opium finally led to a rift with the Wordsworths that never healed.

By 1808, Dove Cottage had become far too small for the Wordsworths and their extended family, which now included poet Thomas De Quincey. Wordsworth had composed some of his greatest poems in the cottage, including 'Intimations of Immortality from Recollections

Wordsworths could no longer bear the sight of their graves in the churchyard.

Wordsworth lived at Rydal Mount for the rest of his life. As his fame grew, so did the number of distinguished visitors who flocked to Rydal Mount to meet him, including Matthew Arnold, Nathaniel

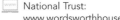
▲ Wordsworth lived at Rydal Mount for 37 years during which time he wrote many poems that established his reputation as one of the greatest poets of his time.

of Early Childhood', but it was time to leave. They moved to Allan Bank, a house at the foot of Easedale, where Coleridge and De Quincey stayed with them briefly. In the spring of 1809, the Wordsworths leased Dove Cottage for De Quincey, who remained its tenant until 1834.

Rydal Mount and Dora's Field

In 1813 William, Mary and their three surviving children moved to Rydal Mount in Ambleside. Two of their children had died in 1812, during their tenancy of the Old Rectory opposite St Oswald's church in Grasmere, and the

Hawthorne and the poet Algernon Swinburne who was only 11 at the time.

Wordsworth was made Poet Laureate in 1843. He died seven years later after catching a chill and was buried in St Oswald's churchyard.

Rydal Mount is now open to visitors. The main bedroom gives a good view of neighbouring Dora's Field, which is a stretch of land that Wordsworth passed to his daughter. It is now planted with thousands of daffodils, which erupt each spring in a flowery riot that evokes the first line of one of Wordsworth's most famous poems, 'I wandered lonely as a cloud'.

ⓘ information

Contact details

Wordsworth House
Main Street
Cockermouth
Cumbria, CA13 9RX

☎ +44 (0)1900 820884

National Trust:
www.wordsworthhouse.org.uk

Transport links

Maryport
Workington

The A594 passes through Cockermouth and the A66 and the A595 pass by

BEATRIX POTTER'S CUMBRIA

CUMBRIA

See map p. 117 ②

KEY FIGURE: Beatrix Potter
KEY LOCATIONS: Near Sawrey; Hill Top; The Tower Bank Arms; Castle Farm

Beatrix Potter (shown opposite) first visited the Lake District in 1882 when she was 16, and it was the start of a lifelong love affair with this part of England. It was sheer chance that brought her here. She and her parents usually spent their summers in Scotland, but when the house they normally rented became unavailable they opted for Cumbria instead. They returned in following years, during which Beatrix gained a vivid impression of the area by watching and sketching the wildlife and the countryside. The charm of

▼ *Beatrix Potter's* The Tale of Benjamin Bunny *was inspired by her first pet rabbit, Benjamin Bouncer.*

THIS is what those little rabbits saw round that corner!

Little Benjamin took one look, and then, in half a minute less than no time, he hid himself and Peter and the onions underneath a large basket . . .

the Lake District inspired Beatrix to write stories about it, and her first book, *The Tale of Peter Rabbit*, was published in 1902. Two more books, *The Tailor of Gloucester* and *Squirrel Nutkin*, swiftly followed in 1903. All of these books were both written and illustrated by her.

Beatrix now had an income of her own, and in 1903 she bought a field in Near Sawrey, where she and her family had stayed on their holiday that year. In 1905, she used the royalties from *The Tale of Peter Rabbit* to buy the small farm of Hill Top. Beatrix lived and worked here for the next eight years, and Hill Top was the home of both Tom Kitten in *The Tale of Tom Kitten* (1907) and Samuel Whiskers in *The Tale of Samuel Whiskers* (1908), while the local pub, The Tower Bank Arms, appeared in *The Tale of Jemima Puddle-Duck* (1908).

Hill Top was Beatrix's artistic inspiration, but it also provided her with a means of gradually separating herself from her family's tight grasp. In October 1913, when she was 47, she married her solicitor, William Heelis, much to the opposition of her parents who made it plain that they believed her rightful duty was to look after them. The couple lived in Castle Farm, which

Beatrix had bought in 1909, but she continued to work at her adored Hill Top.

However, Beatrix's love of farming left her with little time for writing and painting, and she only wrote four more books in her lifetime. The phenomenal and continuing success of her children's stories enabled her to buy a total of 4,000 acres of land, plus 15 farms in which she encouraged the breeding of Herdwick sheep. This rare breed is indigenous to the Lake District, and in 1943 Beatrix achieved the remarkable feat of becoming the first woman to be elected President of the Herdwick Sheepbreeders' Association; however, she died in the same year, before she could take up her position.

On her death, Beatrix Potter left all her land to the National Trust. It was a charity dear to her heart and, interestingly enough, one of the founders was Canon Hardwicke Rawnsley, who was the local vicar when Beatrix first visited the Lake District and who encouraged her to publish her stories. Hill Top was also part of her bequest to the National Trust, with the condition that it should be left exactly as it was when she resided there, and perhaps it is this comfortable,

homely atmosphere that has made it one of the most popular tourist attractions in the entire Lake District.

(i) information

Contact details

Hill Top
Near Sawrey
Hawkshead
Ambleside
Cumbria, LA22 0LF

National Trust:
www.nationaltrust.org.uk/main/
w-hilltop

☎ +44 (0)1539 436269

Transport links

Windermere

The A591 passes through Windermere and the B5285 passes through Hawkshead

LAKE WINDERMERE AND CONISTON WATER

CUMBRIA

See map p. 117 ③

KEY FIGURES: Arthur Ransome; W.G. Collingwood; John Ruskin
KEY LOCATIONS: Blakeholme; Peel Island; Brantwood; Ruskin Museum

Cumbria's Lake District has inspired poets and novelists for centuries, whether they visited the area on precious holidays or actually lived here. Arthur Ransome, the children's author, was born in Leeds, but his father carried him up Coniston Old Man when he was only a few weeks old and it was the start of his lifelong love affair with the area. As a small boy he attended a preparatory school called Old College in Windermere; he went on to attend Rugby (see page 103) and enjoyed family holidays around High Nibthwaite. From these cosy beginnings Ransome went on to become an intrepid traveller and journalist who covered the Russian Revolution first-hand and whose second wife, Evgenia Shelepina, who was once Trotsky's secretary.

Ransome was already a published author when he began *Swallows and Amazons* (1930), which was his first novel for children. It covered what was then the unusual topic of children's holidays and was a slow seller, as was *Swallowdale*, which was published in 1931. Ransome's persistence finally paid off with

▲ *Early in his career, Arthur Ransome worked part-time as foreign correspondent for* The Guardian.

the publication of *Peter Duck* in 1932, and he suddenly found that he was the celebrated author of a best-selling series. He wrote 12 children's novels chronicling the adventures of the Swallow (Walker) and Amazon (Blackett) families, who spent much of their time in the

▲ *Arthur Ransome learnt to sail on Coniston Water while he was attending the school in the town of Windermere.*

Lake District. Although Ransome never specified the location of 'that great lake in the North', it is an amalgam of Lake Windermere and Coniston Water. Equally, Wild Cat Island appears to be a mixture of Blakeholme in Lake Windermere and Peel Island in Coniston Water.

One of Ransome's friends was W. G. Collingwood, secretary to John Ruskin, who was one of the greatest Victorian critics, poets and artists. Both Ruskin and Collingwood lived on Coniston Water, although Ruskin's house, Brantwood, was by far the finer of the two with its magnificent views of the lake.

Ruskin lived at Brantwood, which is now open to the public, from 1871 until his death in 1900. He is buried in St Andrew's churchyard, Coniston, under a tall cross of Tilberthwaite stone, which was designed by Collingwood. Collingwood set up the Ruskin Museum in Coniston, in honour of his friend.

ⓘ information

Contact details

Windermere
Cumbria
LA23

+44 (0)1539 446499

🌐 Local Information:
www.visitcumbria.com/
amb/coniston-water.htm

Transport links

🚉 Windermere
Newby Bridge

🚗 The A5084 and A593 run along Coniston Water and the A592 and A591 run along Lake Windermere

LIVERPOOL
MERSEYSIDE

See map p.117 **4**

KEY FIGURES: William Cobbett; Thomas Paine; Charles Dickens; Liverpool Poets
KEY LOCATIONS: St George's Hall Concert Room; Theatre Royal

In 1819 William Cobbett (1763–1835) arrived at the port of Liverpool with the bones of his great hero, Thomas Paine. Cobbett felt compelled to transport the remains back to England, after Paine had been buried in unconsecrated ground at his farm near New York in 1809. Plans for a memorial were abandoned, however, and his remains later lost.

Other transatlantic travellers who visited Liverpool included Mrs Harriet Beecher Stowe (1811–96), who stayed at Dingle Bank in 1853, and Herman Melville (1819–91), who had spent some time in Liverpool in 1837, and returned in 1856 before sailing to Constantinople.

Charles Dickens also has strong ties to the city, performing at such key venues as St George's Hall Concert Room and the Theatre Royal.

Many successful literary figures were born in Liverpool, including Beryl Bainbridge

▲ *The role of Liverpool's docks inspired Nicholas Monsarrat (1910–79) to write* The Cruel Sea *(1951).*

(1934–2010), Willy Russell (born 1947) and Alan Bleasdale (born 1946).

In the early 1960s, Liverpool was cultivating a trio of poets: Brian Patten (born 1946), Roger McGough (born 1937) and Adrian Henri (1932–2000), collectively known as the Liverpool Poets. The three of them were awarded the Freedom of the City of Liverpool in 2002.

(i) information

Contact details

Liverpool
Merseyside

Local Information:
www.visitliverpool.com

Transport links

Liverpool Central
Liverpool Lime Street

The A57, A59, M57 and M62 run near Liverpool

MANCHESTER
GREATER MANCHESTER

See map p.117 ⑤

KEY FIGURES: Elizabeth Gaskell
KEY LOCATION: 87 Plymouth Grove

The birthplace of Thomas de Quincey, Howard Jacobson and Anthony Burgess, among others, the city of Manchester has also become memorable through the literature of poets such as Shelley, who immortalized the 1819 Peterloo Massacre in 'The Masque of the Anarchy'. The city is most probably best-known through the literature of the writer Elizabeth Gaskell, whose masterpieces *Mary Barton* (1848; shown right) and *North and South* (1855) evoke the grim and unrelenting poverty of 19th-century industrial Manchester. She also sympathetically portrays the bitter existence of people working there and the divide in the class system at the time.

Mrs Gaskell drew on her own experiences of working with her husband, minister William Gaskell, in the city's poorest districts, particularly in writing *Mary Barton*. The novel was written after the death of the Gaskells' son, when William encouraged his wife to pour her grief into her writing. She attracted many fans, including Charles Dickens. Mrs Gaskell's home, a Regency villa at 87 Plymouth Grove, has undergone substantial renovation and reopened in 2011. She lived here with William and their four children from 1850 and wrote all but her first novel here.

The Gaskells entertained several writers at the house, including Charles Dickens, Charlotte Brontë, John Ruskin and Harriet Beecher Stowe.

ⓘ information

Contact details

Manchester
Greater Manchester

☎ Tourist Information:
+44 (0)8712 228223

🖥 Local Information:
www.visitmanchester.com

Elizabeth Gaskell Society:
www.gaskellsociety.co.uk

Transport links

🚆 Manchester Piccadilly

🚌 The M60 and M602 run near Manchester and the A57 (M) and A6042/A665 circle the city

BRONTE PARSONAGE MUSEUM
WEST YORKSHIRE

See map p.117 (6)

KEY FIGURES: Charlotte, Anne, Emily and Branwell Brontë
KEY LOCATION: Haworth Parsonage

The village of Hawarth in West Yorkshire is surely one of the most romantic literary settings in Britain. It conjures up images of a troubled family to whom death was no stranger, but which proved a fertile breeding ground for the talents of Charlotte (1816–55), Anne (1820–49), Emily (1818–48) and Branwell (1817–48) Brontë. There are reminders of these many family tragedies in the graveyard and church, where all the Brontë family lie with the exception of Anne who was buried in Scarborough where she died (see page 130).

COLLINS CLASSICS

CHARLOTTE BRONTË
Jane Eyre

The Brontë siblings grew up in Haworth Parsonage, where their father was perpetual curate. Their mother, Maria, died of cancer in 1821 and was buried in the church. In 1825, she was joined there by her two eldest daughters, Maria and Elizabeth, who both died of consumption. This disease was the scourge of the 19th century, and it flourished in the chilly, damp northern climate.

The three remaining Brontë daughters all worked as governesses, but their real love was writing. They first ventured into print in 1846, with a collection of poems which was published at their own expense under the pseudonyms of Currer, Ellis and Acton Bell. Although they sold only two copies, it acted as a creative catalyst for them and triggered a fever of writing. *Jane Eyre*, by Charlotte (shown left), was published in October 1847 to immediate acclaim, and was followed by Anne's *Agnes Grey* and Emily's *Wuthering Heights* two months later. Anne's second novel, *The Tenant of Wildfell Hall*, was published the following summer. All the novels drew heavily on the sisters' life in Yorkshire, and were considered deeply shocking in some

▲ *After the deaths of her three siblings, Charlotte Brontë was left at Haworth with her father. She had to wait for two years before he gave her permission to marry his curate.*

quarters because they dealt with such themes as adultery, obsessive love and alcoholism. The women had experience of the latter through their brother, Branwell.

The literary outpourings of this tight family group did not last long because both Branwell and Emily died from tuberculosis in 1848, followed by Anne in 1849. Charlotte continued to write novels and in 1854 she married her father's curate, Arthur Bell Nicholls, but she died in March 1855 during the early stages of pregnancy. Her friend, the novelist Mrs Gaskell, published her biography, *Life of Charlotte Brontë*, in 1857.

(i) information

Contact details

The Brontë Parsonage
Museum
Church Street
Haworth, Keighley
West Yorkshire
BD22 8DR

 +44 (0)1535 642323

Brontë Parsonage Museum:
www.bronte.org.uk

Transport links

Ingrow West
Keighley

The B6142 runs through
Haworth and the A629
is nearby

THE OLD SWAN HOTEL
NORTH YORKSHIRE

See map p.117 (7)

KEY FIGURE: Agatha Christie
KEY LOCATIONS: Harrogate; The Old Swan Hotel

In December 1926, Agatha Christie's Morris Cowley was found at Newlands Corner, near Guildford in Surrey, but there was no trace of the novelist (see right) herself. The story was splashed all over the press and the police interviewed her husband Colonel Archie Christie on suspicion of murder. Word reached the *Daily News* that Agatha was, in fact, staying in Yorkshire at the Harrogate Hydro (today The Old Swan Hotel), using the name of Mrs Teresa Neele. The press flocked to the hotel, but her husband did not let her speak to them, excusing her behaviour as 'amnesia'.

This excuse was far from the truth. Colonel Christie was having an affair with a Miss Nancy Neele, and had asked Agatha for a divorce on the morning of her disappearance. The Christies divorced in 1928 and the Colonel married Nancy Neele a few weeks later.

(i) information

Contact details

The Old Swan Hotel
Swan Road
Harrogate
North Yorkshire, HG1 2SR

☎ +44 (0)1423 500055

🌐 The Old Swan Hotel:
www.classiclodges.co.uk/The_
Old_Swan_Hotel_Harrogate

Transport links

🚆 Harrogate

🚌 The A61 and the A6040 run by Harrogate

SHANDY HALL

NORTH YORKSHIRE

See map p.117 (8)

KEY FIGURE: Laurence Sterne
KEY LOCATIONS: Shandy Hall; St Michael's Church

When Laurence Sterne (1713–68) called his new home Shandy Hall, he was being ironic – the building was a medieval priest's house that had been extended in the 17th century. His books, most of which he wrote in the study (shown right) at Shandy Hall, also caused quite a rumpus.

Sterne moved here in 1760 when he was made perpetual curate of St Michael's Church, Coxwold. The first two volumes of his first novel, *The Life and Opinions of Tristram Shandy*, had been published the previous year and he was still enjoying their success and notoriety. Sterne stirred up further moral outrage in 1760 with the publication of *The Sermons of Mr Yorick* (a character from the previous novel) followed by further volumes of Tristram Shandy in 1761, 1765 and 1767. The novel was an art form still in its infancy when Sterne was writing, yet this digressive, self-referential and endlessly inventive book anticipates many of the novelistic innovations of the 20th century. Shandy Hall fell into disrepair, but it was lovingly rescued in the 1960s and restored to its 18th-century appearance.

ⓘ information

Contact details

Shandy Hall
Coxwold
York
YO61 4AD

☎ +44 (0)1347 868465

🖳 The Laurence Sterne Trust:
www.laurencesternetrust.org.uk

Transport links

🚆 Thirsk

🚗 The A19 and A170
run near Coxwold

SCARBOROUGH
NORTH YORKSHIRE

See map p. 117 **9**

KEY FIGURES: Anne Brontë; Edith, Osbert and Sacheverell Sitwell; Susan Hill
KEY LOCATIONS: Belvoir Terrace; St Mary's Church; Londesborough Lodge

In the spring of 1849, Anne Brontë visited Scarborough with her sister, Charlotte, and her friend, Ellen Nussey. Although Anne loved to visit the seaside town for pleasure, this time she had come in a last-ditch attempt to stave off tuberculosis. On 28 May 1849, she died at 2 The Cliff, a building that has since been demolished to make way for the Grand Hotel. She was buried in St Mary's churchyard.

Another important literary family is linked with Scarborough. The Sitwell siblings, Edith (1887–1964), Osbert (1892–1969) and Sacheverell (1897–1988), knew the town well as children because their mother's family owned a house here, Londesborough Lodge. In 1887, Edith was born next door in Wood End, The Crescent, which was her parents' seaside home. Edith's younger brother, Sacheverell, was born 10 years later in Belvoir Terrace.

▲ *Sir Osbert Sitwell arranged to have a copy of his novel* Before the Bombardment *buried with him.*

In 1942 the novelist Susan Hill was born in Scarborough and she wrote about the town in *A Change for the Better* (1969) and in *Family* (1989).

Scarborough is synonymous with the Stephen Joseph Theatre, where Alan Ayckbourn (born 1939) is the artistic director.

ⓘ information

Contact details

Scarborough
North Yorkshire

🌐 Local Information:
www.discoveryorkshire
coast.com

Transport links

🚆 Scarborough

🚌 The A165 and A171 run through Scarborough

WHITBY
NORTH YORKSHIRE

See map p.117 (10)

KEY FIGURES: Bram Stoker; Elizabeth Gaskell; Lewis Carroll
KEY LOCATIONS: Whitby Bay; St Mary's Church; Barnard's Hotel

Legend has it that Bram Stoker (1847–1912) conceived the idea for his Gothic chiller, *Dracula* (1897; shown right), when he was sitting on the cliffs above Whitby Bay. He watched a ship sailing into the harbour and immediately his imaginative processes started working – here was the ship that would bring Count Dracula to England from Transylvania and enable him to turn the innocent Lucy into a fellow member of the 'Un-Dead'.

In the novel, Dracula disembarks in the shape of a large black dog and heads for St Mary's churchyard, which is a favourite sitting place of Mina, a young woman on whom Dracula has designs. Stoker's novel was influenced by 'Carmilla', a short story about a female vampire from *In A Glass Darkly* (1872) by Sheridan Le Fanu (1814–73), and in its turn *Dracula* launched a flourishing industry of vampire films and books that continues to this day.

Whitby had already appeared in print when *Dracula* was published. Mrs Gaskell wrote about the town in *Sylvia's Lovers* (1863), although she called it Monkshaven, and changed the name of St Mary's Church to St Nicholas. She knew the town well after spending two weeks at 1 Abbey Terrace in 1859.

The Reverend Charles Lutwidge Dodgson (Lewis Carroll) was another Victorian visitor to the town. He came here several times between 1854 and 1871, and his poem 'The Walrus and The Carpenter' is said to have been inspired by the beach. He stayed at what is now Barnard's Hotel in East Terrace.

(i) information

Contact details
Whitby
North Yorkshire

Local Information:
www.whitby.co.uk

Transport links
Lealholm

The A170 runs near Whitby

DURHAM CATHEDRAL
COUNTY DURHAM

See map p. 117 (11)

KEY FIGURES: St Cuthbert; Venerable Bede
KEY LOCATION: Durham Cathedral

This is the resting place of both St Cuthbert (died 687) and the Venerable Bede (*c.*673–735), and therefore contains the bones of the chronicled and the chronicler respectively. St Cuthbert was the 7th-century Bishop of Lindisfarne who preferred the life of a hermit to that of an evangelist but accepted the task he had been given. He died on the island of Inner Farne and was buried in Lindisfarne.

When the monks fled Lindisfarne during the Viking raids of 875 they obeyed St Cuthbert's wishes to take his bones with them, and his remains were taken to Durham where a church was built especially for them. This church evolved into Durham Cathedral (shown right), which was built between 1093 and 1135. The saint lies beneath the grey tomb that is inscribed 'Cuthbertus'.

St Bede spent most of his life in St Paul's monastery at his home town of Jarrow.

His most famous book is his *Historia Ecclesiastica Gentis Anglorum*, or *Ecclesiastical History of the English People*, which he completed in 731.

(i) information

Contact details

The Chapter Office
The College
Durham, DH1 3EH

☎ +44 (0)1913 864266

Durham Cathedral:
www.durhamcathedral.co.uk

Transport links

Durham

The A66(M) and A194(M) run through Durham

THE MORDEN TOWER

TYNE AND WEAR

See map p.117 (12)

KEY FIGURES: Basil Bunting; Ted Hughes; Seamus Heaney; Allen Ginsberg
KEY LOCATION: The Morden Tower

The Morden Tower has nestled in the West Walls of the city of Newcastle-upon-Tyne since it was built in about 1290. Despite having survived for so long it was in a terrible state when it was leased as a venue for poetry readings in 1964. After it was repaired, the round upper room in the tower became an important showcase for many leading poets.

In December 1965, Basil Bunting (1900–85) gave the first reading of his semi-autobiographical poem, *Briggflatts*, which was published the following year. He already had a strong following as a modernist poet in other countries, thanks to the publication of *Redimiculum Matellarum* (1930) in Milan and *Poems* (1950) in Texas, but failed to make much impact on British poetry fans until *Briggflatts* appeared in print.

A string of poets followed Bunting to the Morden Tower, including Poet Laureate Ted

▲ *Poets including Ted Hughes have enthralled audiences at the Tower, which seats only 50 people.*

Hughes (1930–98), Seamus Heaney (born 1939), Allen Ginsberg (1926–97), who in the 1960s declared that Liverpool was 'the centre of consciousness for the entire human universe', and the Liverpool Poets – Brian Patten, Adrian Henri and Roger McGough.

(i) information

Contact details

Back Stowell Street
West Walls
Newcastle Upon Tyne
Tyne and Wear
NE1 4XG

Morden Tower Association:
www.mordentower.org

Transport links

Newcastle

The A167 (M) runs through
Newcastle Upon Tyne

SCOTLAND

Scotland has a very strong literary tradition in both Gaelic and English. The beauty and diversity of the country's landscape and the gritty urban reality of its cities have inspired many of the famous and influential authors who lived and wrote here – from Sir Walter Scott and Sir Arthur Conan Doyle to J.K. Rowling and Ian Rankin. The buildings, museums, cafés and monuments of Edinburgh and Glasgow, in particular, reflect the nation's literary history. Sir Walter Scott's statue in Princes Street looks out over Edinburgh and his collection of 'Waverley' novels gave its name to the city's main railway station. Robert Burns also has many connections with the city and with other parts of Scotland, such as Alloway where he was born. Glasgow appears as a backdrop to the novels of writers as diverse as A.J. Cronin, John Buchan and Alistair Maclean. The wild coastline has attracted writers of every ilk – from George Orwell, who spent his last years on the Isle of Jura, and Gavin Maxwell, who enjoyed the final years of his life with his otters at Sandaig overlooking the Isle of Skye.

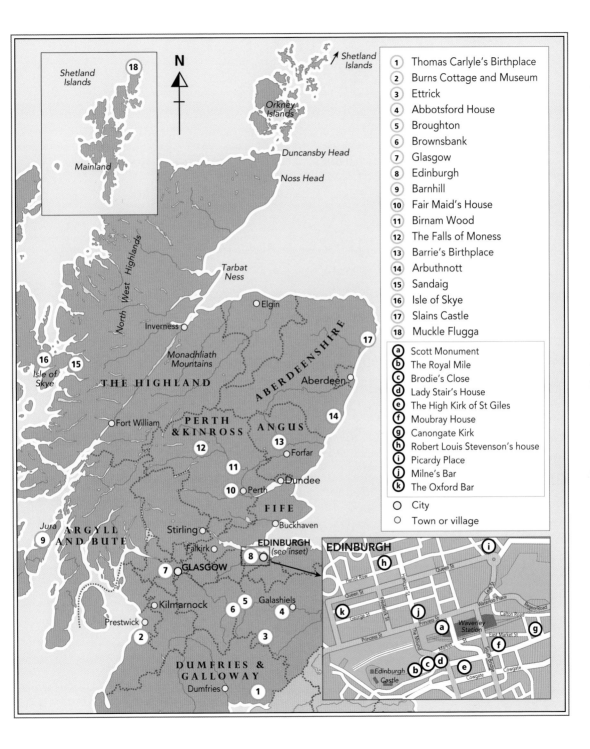

N

①	Thomas Carlyle's Birthplace
②	Burns Cottage and Museum
③	Ettrick
④	Abbotsford House
⑤	Broughton
⑥	Brownsbank
⑦	Glasgow
⑧	Edinburgh
⑨	Barnhill
⑩	Fair Maid's House
⑪	Birnam Wood
⑫	The Falls of Moness
⑬	Barrie's Birthplace
⑭	Arbuthnott
⑮	Sandaig
⑯	Isle of Skye
⑰	Slains Castle
⑱	Muckle Flugga

ⓐ	Scott Monument
ⓑ	The Royal Mile
ⓒ	Brodie's Close
ⓓ	Lady Stair's House
ⓔ	The High Kirk of St Giles
ⓕ	Moubray House
ⓖ	Canongate Kirk
ⓗ	Robert Louis Stevenson's house
ⓘ	Picardy Place
ⓙ	Milne's Bar
ⓚ	The Oxford Bar

O City
○ Town or village

Shetland Islands

Shetland Islands

Mainland

Orkney Islands

Duncansby Head

Noss Head

Tarbat Ness

North West Highlands

Elgin

Inverness

Monadhliath Mountains

ABERDEENSHIRE

THE HIGHLAND

Aberdeen

Isle of Skye

Fort William

PERTH &KINROSS

ANGUS

Forfar

Dundee

Perth

FIFE

Buckhaven

Jura

ARGYLL AND BUTE

Stirling

Falkirk

EDINBURGH (see inset)

Kilmarnock

Galashiels

GLASGOW

Prestwick

DUMFRIES & GALLOWAY

Dumfries

EDINBURGH

Heriot Row

Queen St

Queen St

Leith St

Waterloo Place

Regent Road

George St

Frederick St

Hanover St

Princes St

The Mound

Waverley Station

Calton Road

East Market St

South Bridge

Princes St

Market St

Cowgate

Edinburgh Castle

Cowgate

THOMAS CARLYLE'S BIRTHPLACE

DUMFRIES AND GALLOWAY

See map p.135 (1)

KEY FIGURE: Thomas Carlyle
KEY LOCATIONS: Arched House, Ecclefechan

Thomas Carlyle was born in 1795 in the Arched House in Ecclefechan. The young Thomas grew up in a powerfully Calvinist atmosphere, which had a major influence on him. His parents educated him at home until he was five, after which he attended the village school, progressing to the Annan Academy when he was nine. He studied at the University of Edinburgh before returning to Annan, where he taught from 1814 to 1816. He continued to teach after leaving Annan and also started to write. Carlyle's *Life of Schiller* was published in the *London Magazine* in 1823–24, and appeared in book form in 1825.

In 1826, he married Jane Baillie Welsh and the couple began their married life in Edinburgh, before moving to Jane's farm in Craigenputtock.

In 1834, the Carlyles moved to Cheyne Row in London, where they remained for the rest of their lives. Carlyle's literary career took off at this point with the publication in 1833–34 of *Sartor Resartus*. When Carlyle died in 1881 he was known as the 'sage of Chelsea', and was so respected that straw was put down in the street so that noise from the passing horses' hooves would not disturb the dying man.

Although Carlyle could have been buried at Westminster Abbey, he wanted to lie in the Ecclefechan churchyard, beside his parents. A statue was erected in his memory in the village in 1927. The Arched House is now a museum replete with Carlyle's belongings and memorabilia.

(i) information

Contact details

Thomas Carlyle's Birthplace
The Arched House
Ecclefechan
Dumfries and Galloway
DG11 3DG

National Trust:
www.nts.org.uk/Property/60

☎ +44 (0)844 493 2247

Transport links

Lockerbie

The A47(M) runs by Ecclefechan and the B725 runs through

BURNS COTTAGE & MUSEUM

SOUTH AYRSHIRE

See map p. 135 (2)

KEY FIGURE: Robert Burns

KEY LOCATIONS: Burns Cottage; Alloway; Burns National Heritage Park

On 25 January each year, Scottish households traditionally commemorate with haggis and whisky an event that took place in a whitewashed, thatched cottage in Ayr in 1759 – the birth of Scottish Baird Robert Burns (shown right). The eldest of seven children, the young Robert grew up in a two-room building that his father, William, had built himself in 1757. In 1766, William became a tenant farmer, first at Mount Oliphant near Alloway and, in 1777, at Lochlie Farm, Tarbolton. His son helped him whenever his schoolwork allowed. However, poor harvests and overwork took their toll on William and he died in 1784. He was buried in Alloway Kirk, which is where Robert Burns later set much of his poem 'Tam o' Shanter'.

The Burns family moved to Mossgiel Farm, near Mauchline. It was a formative time for Robert, during which he wrote several poems, including 'To A Mouse', 'Holy Willie's Prayer', 'The Jolly Beggars' and 'The Holy Fair'. His first collection of poems, *Poems, Chiefly in the Scottish Dialect* (1786) was extremely popular, but he could not afford to leave farming and later moved to Ellisland Farm, near Dumfries, with his wife, Jean Armour, and their two children.

Burns Cottage in Alloway is open to the public. In Alloway there is the Burns National Heritage Park, which includes the Burns Monument.

(i) information

Contact details

Murdoch's Lone
Alloway
Ayr, KA7 4PQ

☎ +44 (0)844 493 2601

[www] Burns Cottage and Museum:
www.burnsmuseum.org.uk

Transport links

🚃 Ayr

🚗 The A77 runs near Alloway and the B7024 runs through

ETTRICK

BORDERS

See map p.135 ③

KEY FIGURES: James Hogg; Sir Walter Scott
KEY LOCATIONS: Tibbie Shiels Inn; Gordon Arms; Aikwood Tower; Scott's Courtroom

A tall monument decorated with a bronze medallion marks the birthplace of the Scottish poet James Hogg. Born in 1770, he grew up in Ettrick and left school aged seven after his father went bankrupt. The young James became a cowherd and later a shepherd. Astonishingly, Hogg was later able to combine working as a shepherd with a career as a professional writer.

Hogg eventually met Sir Walter Scott (shown above) who was looking for material to include in *Minstrelsy of the Scottish Border* (1802). Scott liked what Hogg sent him and encouraged him to write more. After Hogg's early poems were published in *The Mountain Bard* (1807) he made his name with *The Queen's Wake* (1813). Hogg also wrote novels, including *The Private Memoirs and Confessions of a Justified Sinner* (1824).

He remained close to Scott, and often met him at Tibbie Shiels Inn between St Mary's Loch and Loch of the Lowes. According to legend, Scott and Hogg's last meeting was held at the Gordon Arms Hotel, near Mountbenger, where fragments of some of Scott's letters decorate the walls of the bar.

After Scott died in 1832, Hogg wrote *The Domestic Manners and Private Life of Sir Walter Scott* (1834). Hogg died the following year, prompting William Wordsworth to write 'Upon the Death of James Hogg' in tribute. Hogg is now remembered in many places around Ettrick, and there is an exhibition dedicated to him at Aikwood Tower near Ettrickbridge, as well as some information about him in Scott's Courtroom (now a museum) in Selkirk.

ⓘ information

Contact details
Ettrick
The Scottish Borders
TD7

Transport links
🚆 Lockerbie closest, 26 miles

🚗 The A702, the A74(M) and the A7 run near Ettrick

ABBOTSFORD HOUSE

BORDERS

See map p.135 (4)

KEY FIGURE: Sir Walter Scott
KEY LOCATION: Melrose

Sir Walter Scott spent 13 years converting Abbotsford House into a romantic, Scottish baronial fantasy that was the architectural equivalent of his many novels. Built on the site of Cartley Hole Farm in Melrose, the first incarnation of the house was built between 1816 and 1818. During this time, Scott began to buy adjoining parcels of land, which made the house seem small. Scott's many guests, who included the writer Washington Irving and the painter J.M.W. Turner, did not help the situation.

When Scott was awarded a baronetcy in 1818 he decided he had to live in a much grander house, which his builders completed in 1824. He took advances from his publisher and borrowed from his printer to help fund the build, but ended up with a total debt of £120,000. He did not lose the house however, as he put it in his son's name.

▲ *Sir Walter Scott referred to his home that was rebuilt at great expense as 'Conundrum Castle'.*

Abbotsford is open to the public and visitors can see the study where he wrote so many of his bestsellers and which contains over 9,000 rare volumes, and the dining room where Scott died.

(i) information

Contact details

The Abbotsford Trust
Abbotsford, Melrose
Roxburghshire
TD6 9BQ

[www] Scott's Abbotsford
www.scottsabbotsford.co.uk

☎ +44 (0)1896 752043

Transport links

🚗 The A7 and the A6091 run through Abbotsford; the B6360 runs near the Trust

BROUGHTON
SOUTH LANARKSHIRE

See map p.135 ⑤

KEY FIGURES: John Buchan; O. Douglas
KEY LOCATIONS: Biggar; The John Buchan Centre

The young John Buchan (1875–1940), who later became a novelist, publisher and politician, spent his holidays in Biggar at his grandparents' house, The Green. The town held sentimental memories for his parents, who were married at the Free Church, which is now the John Buchan Centre. Both Buchan and his sister, Anna, found Broughton a source of inspiration. For Buchan, it became Woodilee in *Witch Wood* (1927), while Anna, who wrote as O. Douglas, completed her novel *Penny Plain* (1913) while staying here.

Broughton was not the only place in Scotland to inspire Buchan. It is believed that the steps at Ravenscraig Castle in Fife inspired the title of Buchan's best-known novel *The Thirty-Nine Steps* (1915). These novels eclipsed his biographies of important figures, such as Sir Walter Scott, for which he would have preferred to have been

▲ *The John Buchan Centre in Broughton is full of memorabilia connected with the author.*

known. He did receive the respect he craved in politics: Buchan was Governor General of Canada from 1935 to 1940. When he was awarded a baronetcy, he chose to be known as Baron Tweedsmuir, after the village near Broughton.

ⓘ information

Contact details

Broughton, Biggar
South Lanarkshire
The Scottish Borders

☎ Tourist Information:
+44 (0)1899 221066

💻 Local Information:
www.visitlanarkshire.com

The John Buchan Society:
www.johnbuchansociety.co.uk

Transport links

🚆 Carstairs (12 miles)

🚌 The A701 runs through Broughton

BROWNSBANK

SOUTH LANARKSHIRE

See map p. 135   **6**

KEY FIGURE: Hugh MacDiarmid
KEY LOCATION: Brownsbank

This tiny cottage was the home of Hugh MacDiarmid, one of Scotland's greatest 20th-century poets, from 1951 until his death in 1978. In this cottage he entertained the visitors who flocked to pay homage to the man credited with leading Scotland's literary and cultural revival.

MacDiarmid was the pen name of Christopher Murray Grieve, who was born in Langholm, in Dumfriesshire, in 1892. He developed a political conscience at an early age and in 1928 helped to found the National Party of Scotland, although he was expelled in 1933. A year later he joined the Communist Party, but was expelled from that in 1938. Grieve began to write under his pseudonym in 1922 and his first collection of poetry, *Sangschaw*, was published in 1925. *A Drunk Man Looks at the Thistle*, which is widely considered to be MacDiarmid's greatest work, was published in 1926. In 1931, MacDiarmid

Hugh MacDiarmid's poem, 'The Little White Rose', is engraved by the front door of his cottage.

launched the leftist sympathies of that decade when he wrote *First Hymn to Lenin*, which acted as a clarion call to such poets as C. Day-Lewis, Stephen Spender and W.H. Auden.

MacDiarmid is commemorated on a hill in Langholm by a large metallic sculpture, which is shaped like a book.

ⓘ information

Contact details

Brownsbank, Biggar
South Lanarkshire
ML12 6FJ

☎ +44 (0)1899 860327

Biggar Museum Trust:
www.biggarmuseumtrust.co.uk

Transport links

Carstairs (12 miles)

The A702 runs through Biggar

GLASGOW
CITY OF GLASGOW

See map p.135 (7)

KEY FIGURES: Sir John Betjeman; Sir Walter Scott; Thomas De Quincey; John Buchan; A.J. Cronin; James Boswell; Alistair MacLean

KEY LOCATIONS: George Square; Renfield Street; The Gorbals; Queen Mary Avenue; Glasgow University; Rutherglen

As far as the poet Sir John Betjeman was concerned, Glasgow is 'the greatest Victorian city in the world'. For decades it was considered to be the grimy, rough and poor relation of genteel Edinburgh, with the 'Gorbals Diehards', who appear in some of the novels of John Buchan, forming a stark contrast to the nicely brought up Edinburgh schoolgirls who were described in *The Prime of Miss Jean Brodie* (1961) by Muriel Spark. Nevertheless, Glasgow dusted off its rough, tough image in the 1980s and it is now enjoying a cultural renaissance.

Glasgow's George Square is dominated by a statue of Sir Walter Scott. Statues of other luminaries, such as Robert Burns, the Glaswegian poet Thomas Campbell and Queen Victoria herself, are arranged around the base of the plinth. Thomas De Quincey rented rooms at 79 Renfield Street in the 1840s, although he rarely put in an appearance. He would have been the ideal lodger, but for his growing addiction to opium and his tendency to run out of money.

When John Buchan wrote of the Gorbals Diehards he knew what he was talking about,

▲ *A.J. Cronin was a very productive writer, who averaged 5,000 words per day.*

as he and his sister, Anna, grew up in Glasgow and similar boys had attended John's Sunday school. The Buchan family lived in Queen Mary Avenue until the 1890s, and John and Anna were educated at Hutcheson's Grammar School in the city. John then read law at Glasgow University, during which time he compiled an anthology of the essays of Francis Bacon and wrote his first novel, *Sir Quixote of the Moors*.

A.J. Cronin (1896–1981) was another student of Glasgow University. He read medicine and practised as a doctor for several years until 1930 when he contracted a chronic duodenal ulcer and was advised to rest. He used the time to write and to carry out the research that would form *Hatter's Castle* (1931). The novel, which he wrote in three months, was a triumph and Cronin never returned to medicine. *The Citadel* (1937) is one of his best-known novels, although he is now chiefly remembered as the creator of Dr Finlay of Tannochbrae.

Not every student of the university did well here, or even stayed the course. James Boswell was sent to the university in 1759 by his father, who hoped that it would put paid to his son's unsuitable attachment to an actress. Boswell did not stay long and soon decamped for London, where he was received into the Roman Catholic church. As far as his Calvinist parents were concerned, this was even worse than sleeping with actresses and he was soon persuaded to revert to Protestantism.

Alistair MacLean (1922–87) was born in Glasgow and educated at Hillhead High School.

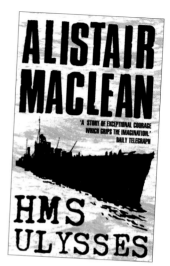

The Second World War interrupted his formal education and he joined the Royal Navy, but this gave him valuable experience when writing the adventure stories that later made him so famous. After the war MacLean attended Glasgow University and graduated in 1953. He taught English at Gallowflat School in Rutherglen in Glasgow and wrote short stories in his spare time.

MacLean's entry into the world of professional writing sounds like a work of fiction in itself because it happened so quickly and smoothly. When one of his stories won a competition in the *Glasgow Herald*, MacLean was commissioned by the Glasgow publishers, William Collins, to write a novel. In 10 weeks he completed *HMS Ulysses* (shown above), which sold over a quarter of a million hardback copies in just six months. In later years MacLean also wrote screenplays, all of which were a success. Many of his books sold over a million copies.

ⓘ information

Contact details

Glasgow
City of Glasgow

Tourist Information:
www.glasgow.gov.uk/en/
Visitors

Transport links

Glasgow Central

The M8, M74 and M77
run through Glasgow

EDINBURGH

CITY OF EDINBURGH

See map p. 135 **8**

KEY FIGURES: Sir Walter Scott; Daniel Defoe; Dr Samuel Johnson; Robert L. Stevenson; Robert Burns; Sir Arthur Conan Doyle; Ian Rankin; J.K. Rowling

KEY LOCATIONS: Scott Monument; Royal Mile; Brodie's Close; Writers' Museum; High Kirk of St Giles; Canongate Kirk; 17 Heriot Row; Picardy Place; Milne's Bar; The Oxford Bar; Nicolson's Café

Scotland's capital city of Edinburgh, or Auld Reekie as it is popularly known, has a long literary tradition stretching back centuries. It is almost impossible to walk its streets without coming across a building, monument or bar associated with a great writer. Several literary walking tours are available and are a very good way to see the city and many of the sites mentioned in this entry. In August each year, tents line the gardens of Charlotte Square on George Street for the literary celebration that is the Edinburgh International Book Festival.

The Scott Monument

Looming over Princes Street Gardens and Princes Street, the Scott Monument (shown right) leaves no doubt about the place that Sir Walter Scott occupied in the collective hearts of Victorian Scotland.

Scott is most famous for his series of 'Waverley' novels, after which Edinburgh's main railway station is named, which were a tremendous success when they were first

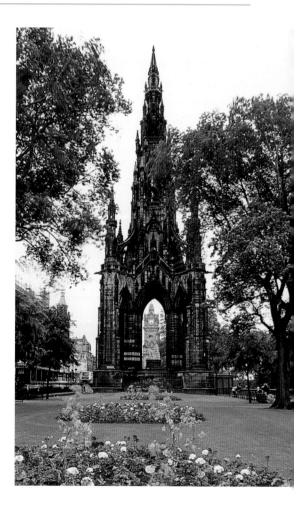

published. In these novels, which included *Waverley* (1814), *Rob Roy* (1817) and *A Legend of Montrose* (1819), Scott's characters were caught up in some of the turbulent events from Scotland's past. The public loved them, although they must have wondered about the true identity of the author, as Scott published them under the unlikely pseudonym of Jebediah Cleisbotham or 'Author of Waverley'.

Scott was born in Edinburgh in August 1771 and he initially embarked on a legal career. He was apprenticed to his father, a solicitor, in 1786 before being called to the bar at the age of 21 in 1792. In 1799 he was appointed Sheriff-Deputy of Selkirk, and in 1806 was also made clerk to the Court of Session in Edinburgh. A chronic shortage of money meant that he had to turn himself into what he described as 'a writing automaton' in order to fund his extravagant, comfortable lifestyle. Such constant pressure eroded his health and he died in 1832.

Four years later a competition was launched to find a suitable design for his monument. Carpenter George Meikle Kemp's plan won in 1838 and the foundation stone was laid on 15 August 1840. The Scott Monument was opened in August 1846 and has been a great tourist attraction ever since. It is carved from Pale Binney sandstone from West Lothian. The central sculpture, depicting Scott accompanied by his deerhound, Maida, was created by Sir John Steell. The monument is decorated with statuettes of 64 characters from Scott's novels, as well as statuettes of 16 Scottish writers. A copy of Scott's statue stands in Central Park, New York, opposite another of Robert Burns.

Visitors can also see the exterior of the house where Scott resided for 28 years at 39 North Castle Street, near George Street.

The Royal Mile

Running from the Palace of Holyroodhouse to Edinburgh Castle, the Royal Mile is actually made up of four streets that form Edinburgh's Old Town: Canongate, High Street, Lawnmarket and Castlehill.

To walk along the Royal Mile is to take a trip into literary history, as so many famous writers have had associations with it. Daniel Defoe, who lived in the Royal Mile in 1707, described it as 'the largest, longest and finest street … in the World'. Allan Ramsay, the 18th-century poet who started the first circulating library in Scotland, had a bookshop in Niddry's Wynd (now Niddry Street) from 1718 to 1726. While he was here he wrote *The Gentle Shepherd* (1725), the pastoral drama for which he is best known. He later moved to Goose Pie House near the castle esplanade, and there is a statue of him in Princes Street Gardens.

Dr Samuel Johnson made his first trip to Edinburgh in 1773, at the start of his long tour of the Hebrides with his friend and later biographer, James Boswell, and stayed in St Mary's Wynd (now St Mary's Street) off Canongate. Boswell himself lived in James Court, off Lawnmarket, for a while but the house was later destroyed in a fire.

Tobias Smollett (1721–71) described Edinburgh in *The Expedition of Humphry Clinker* (1771), after visiting his sister at 182 Canongate in 1766. A plaque on the wall of 22 St John Street commemorates the event.

Thomas De Quincey lived at various addresses in Edinburgh from 1828 until his death in 1859. However, whenever his financial problems became too acute, he moved to the Sanctuary in Holyrood, which was a collection of houses that provided a refuge for debtors.

At the bottom of the Royal Mile lies the Scottish Poetry Library. This great Edinburgh location is housed in a new building near the Scottish Parliament and Holyrood House. Founded in 1984, it has built up an impressive collection of modern and historic poetry from all around the world, as well as verse written especially for Scotland. It also has collections at other locations and a poetry van that travels around the country. The Royal Mile also features in more recent fiction, such as in Ian Rankin's novels.

Brodie's Close

Like any city, Edinburgh has a darker side, characterized by the alleyways or wynds that snake off the Royal Mile and which evoke nefarious deeds. This is the city of Burke and Hare, the notorious 'resurrectionists', as grave-robbers were referred to in Victorian times. In the 1820s, they kept Edinburgh physician Robert Knox supplied with a steady flow of dead bodies, many the corpses of people they had murdered.

▲ *Brodie's Close still conjures up images of Deacon Brodie, whose life inspired Stevenson's Dr Jekyll.*

Such tales fascinated Robert Louis Stevenson, who was born in the city in 1850. One of his short stories was *The Body Snatcher* (1884), which was set in Glencorse Old Church, Lothian.

Another sinister tale that intrigued him was that of Deacon William Brodie, the cabinet-maker who was a staunch member of the Town Council by day and a burglar by night. Brodie's Close was named after his father, Francis, and it is where Deacon Brodie lived until he was forced to escape to the Netherlands. He was caught and returned to Edinburgh, where he was hanged. The story of a man with a personality that is torn between good and evil was the essence of *The Strange Case of Dr Jekyll and Mr Hyde*, which Stevenson wrote in 1886.

Stevenson came from a distinguished family of engineers, against whom he did his best to rebel by visiting brothels while he was at Edinburgh University. Although he initially trained as an engineer, Stevenson soon switched to studying law, before becoming a professional writer. His health was always frail and he spent much of his life searching for a suitable climate in which to live. His travels took him all over the world, feeding his creative imagination, but Scotland was always his greatest source of inspiration.

Lady Stair's House (Writers' Museum)

The atmospheric and evocative location of Lady Stair's House is the ideal setting for the Writers' Museum, which commemorates the literary careers of three of Scotland's greatest writers:

▲ *Robert Burns's writing desk is one of the personal exhibits on display at the Writers' Museum.*

Robert Burns, Sir Walter Scott and Robert Louis Stevenson. The beguiling house is tucked away in Lady Stairs Close and is next to Makars' Court, a monument that is inscribed with quotes of many great Scottish writers. The exhibits inside the house are just as enchanting. They include Scott's chessboard and rocking horse, Stevenson's riding boots and an eerie plaster cast of Burns's skull. It's fitting that Burns should be remembered with such intimacy at the museum as, of the three, he lived closest to it. Burns came to the Scottish capital in the winter of 1786–87, when he was celebrated as the author of *Poems, Chiefly in the Scottish Dialect* (1786). Edinburgh did not suit him, however, and he could not make enough money from his writing, so he returned to farming in Dumfries.

The High Kirk of St Giles

This is the parish church of medieval Edinburgh (shown below), and it was from here that John Knox (*c*.1513–72) orchestrated the Scottish Reformation in the 1550s when he was the minister. He was the author of *First Blast of the Trumpet Against the Monstrous Regiment of Women* (1558), an infamous polemic against Mary, Queen of Scots, which also managed to offend Mary Tudor (the future Mary I), Princess Elizabeth (the future Elizabeth I), and Catherine de Medici of France.

Given the strict morals of John Knox and his fellow Calvinists, it is hardly surprising that there was an uproar when a special window dedicated to the memory of Robert Burns was placed in the church in 1985. Burns's life, full of women and alcohol, was in complete contrast to the ideals of Scottish Presbyterianism.

A pattern set in the cobblestones outside the cathedral in the High Street marks the site of an old tollbooth that has long since vanished. It was built in 1466 and finally demolished in 1817, by which time it was a prison known as the Heart of Midlothian. It was the inspiration for Sir Walter Scott's novel of the same name, which was published in 1818. The book begins in the prison and tells the story of Jeanie Dean, who travels to

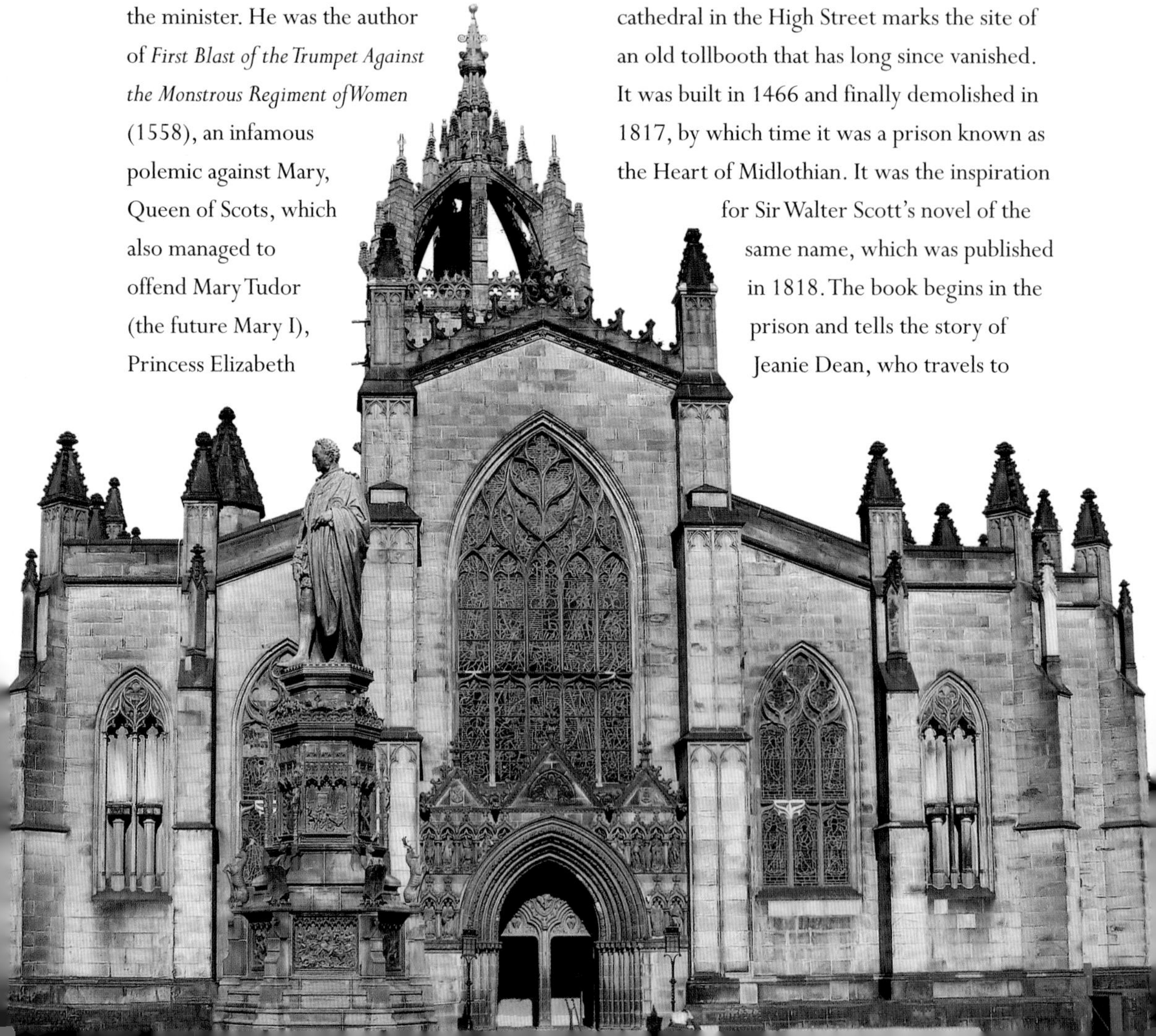

London to appeal on behalf of her sister, who has been wrongly charged with the murder of a child. The novel was based on the true story of Helen Walker.

Canongate Kirk

Completed in 1690, the kirk lies in Canongate near Holyrood House. Its graveyard houses many famous graves, including that of Robert Fergusson. His first collection of poetry was published in 1773 and had a powerful effect on Robert Burns, who was moved to emulate Fergusson's verse. Burns did so in 'The Cotter's Saturday Night', which was inspired by Fergusson's 'The Farmer's Ingle'.

In 1774 Fergusson died at the age of 24 and he lies under a headstone that was donated by Robert Burns in 1786. Burns also wrote Fergusson's epitaph. Among the other writers buried here is economist and *The Wealth of Nations* (1776) author Adam Smith (1723–90).

Robert Louis Stevenson's house

In 1857, Thomas and Margaret Stevenson moved with their young son, Robert, to 17 Heriot Row, in Edinburgh's New Town. Robert Lewis (later Louis) was a sickly child. He was entertained by his adored nurse, Alison

▲ *Robert Louis Stevenson's Dr Jekyll and Mr Hyde reflects the duality of the city of Edinburgh.*

Cunningham, who regaled him with stories about the Scots Presbyterian martyrs, and read to him from the Victorian 'penny-dreadfuls', as the serial novels that were so popular at the time were known.

It was while he was working towards a law degree that Stevenson realized he wanted to be a writer, and he began to write essays before branching out into novels. He particularly enjoyed writing about his travels, publishing several books on the subject, including *An Inland Voyage* (1878) and *Travels with a Donkey in the Cevennes* (1879). Stevenson nursed a broken heart while writing the latter book, as he had met and fallen in love with Fanny Osbourne, a married American woman 10 years older than him. After she sent Stevenson a cablegram in 1879 breaking off their relationship, he

impetuously sailed from Greenock in Scotland
to New York, from where he took the train to
California in the hope that he might manage to
change her mind. The journey nearly killed him,
but he survived and Fanny eventually divorced
her husband. The couple were married in
San Francisco in 1880 and visited Edinburgh so
Fanny could meet her in-laws.

Stevenson was already ill with what is now
thought to be tuberculosis, but he managed
to write some of his most enduring and popular
work after his marriage, including *Treasure Island*
(1883), *Kidnapped* (1886) and *The Strange Case of
Dr Jekyll and Mr Hyde* (1886). In 1888, Stevenson
sailed for the South Seas in the hope of
improving his health, with his wife, his stepson
and his mother. They settled in Samoa, where
Stevenson died in December 1894.

Picardy Place

Another famous Edinburgh writer is Sir Arthur
Conan Doyle, creator of the famous detective
Sherlock Holmes. He was born on 22 May
1859 in Picardy Place and was one of
10 children. He was later educated in Jesuit
schools, studied medicine at Edinburgh
University and practised medicine in the city.
Edinburgh is mentioned in Doyle's books,
including *The Lost World* (1912) in which
Professor Challenger alludes to Salisbury
Craigs. Today an oversized statue of Sherlock
Holmes sits opposite Doyle's birthplace.
Visitors can also have a drink at The Conan
Doyle, a short stroll away in York Place.

▲ *Sir Arthur Conan Doyle based Sherlock Holmes
partly on one of his lecturers at Edinburgh University.*

Milne's Bar

Of the many drinking holes in Edinburgh – and
there are many – Milne's Bar, in Hanover Street,
is probably one of the most famous for its
literary associations. Milne's Bar is also known as
the Poet's Bar, since it was a favourite haunt of
Hugh MacDiarmid, Sorley MacLean, Norman
MacCaig and Sydney Goodsir Smith.

The Oxford Bar

Another bar associated strongly with an author
and also the crime-fiction character who he
created is The Oxford Bar, near Princes Street.
The author Ian Rankin is a local here and the
bar features in the Inspector John Rebus books,
cropping up first in *Mortal Causes* (1994) and

▲ Ian Rankin's books are littered with locations such as the Royal Mile, the Scottish Parliament, the Meadows and Marchmont. Visitors can also go on a Rebus tour of Edinburgh, which calls at The Oxford Bar.

also *The Hanging Garden* (1998). Rebus, like his creator, becomes a local.

Nicolson's Café and Elephant House Café

Magic wands and Quidditch must have seemed like a world away for J.K. Rowling (born 1965) when she moved to Edinburgh in 1993 with her four-month-old daughter, Jessica. As a single parent, life in Edinburgh was tough for Rowling. She was out of work, lived in a tiny flat and was diagnosed with clinical depression. But she found in Edinburgh a charm that fired her imagination to create Harry Potter, one of the most famous children's book characters of all time. Nicolson's Café on North Bridge and the Elephant House Café on George IV Bridge were creative hubs for Rowling and she would write for hours on end while the young Jessica slept by her side.

Millions of children and adults around the globe have become enchanted by the magical world Rowling created and the last four installments in the series consecutively broke the record for the fastest-selling book of all time.

ⓘ information

Contact details

Edinburgh
City of Edinburgh

🖥 Tourist Information:
www.edinburgh.org

Edinburgh UNESCO
City of Literature:
www.cityofliterature.com

Transport links

🚆 Edinburgh Central
Edinburgh Waverley

🚗 The M8 and M9 run into
Edinburgh, as does the A702.

BARNHILL
ARGYLL

See map p. 135 ⑨

KEY FIGURE:	George Orwell
KEY LOCATION:	Isle of Jura

In 1945 George Orwell (shown right) visited the Isle of Jura. The literary triumph of *Animal Farm* (1945) had been overshadowed by Orwell's grief at the death of his wife, Eileen, that same year. Her death was made more bitter by the fact that the Orwells had adopted a baby son, Richard, only the year before.

The move to Jura enabled Orwell to concentrate on work as a means of coping with his bereavement. His friends noticed that he seemed ill and emaciated, and shortly after the move he began to show obvious signs of tuberculosis, although he did his best to ignore these. Living in his cottage, Barnhill, was a success and he delighted in exploring the countryside and examining the wildlife. He also began his final novel, *Nineteen Eighty-Four* (1949), while here, although it gave him more trouble than he had anticipated – he referred to it as 'that bloody book'. There were also distractions in the shape of visitors, boat trips and the many delights of summer in the Inner Hebrides.

By the autumn of 1947 his work was also held up by a recurrence of tuberculosis, which led to enforced bed-rest at Barnhill. The novel was finished by the end of 1948 but so was Orwell's stamina, and in January 1949 he took his final journey south to a sanatorium in the Cotswolds, from where he was later moved to University College Hospital, London. He died in hospital in January 1950, five days before a planned trip to Switzerland, and is buried in Sutton Courtenay, Oxfordshire.

ⓘ information

Contact details

Barnhill
Inverlussa
Isle Of Jura
PA60 7XW

🌐 Travel Information:
www.jurainfo.com

Transport links

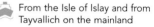

🚢 From the Isle of Islay and from Tayvallich on the mainland

✈ Islay

FAIR MAID'S HOUSE

PERTHSHIRE

See map p. 135 (10)

KEY FIGURE:	Sir Walter Scott
KEY LOCATION:	Fair Maid's House

It is largely thanks to Sir Walter Scott, the aptly named Scottish author, that Scotland's history is celebrated in the way it is today.

When Scott started to write *The Fair Maid of Perth* (1828), he chose a house on the corner of Blackfriars Wynd in Perth as the home of Catherine Glover, his heroine. This is now known as Fair Maid's House, in honour of the book. A bloodthirsty tale of rivalry in love, the novel was set in late 14th-century Perth and was Scott's final major literary success. After it was published Scott wrote in his journal 'I can spin a tough yarn still'.

Scott continued to write until his death in 1832 but he never again achieved the acclaim he received for *The Fair Maid of Perth*.

Today Perth's oldest secular building, Fair Maid's House spent many years in serious disrepair. It was reopened in July 2011, after £750,000 of investment, as a geographical, educational and visitor's centre.

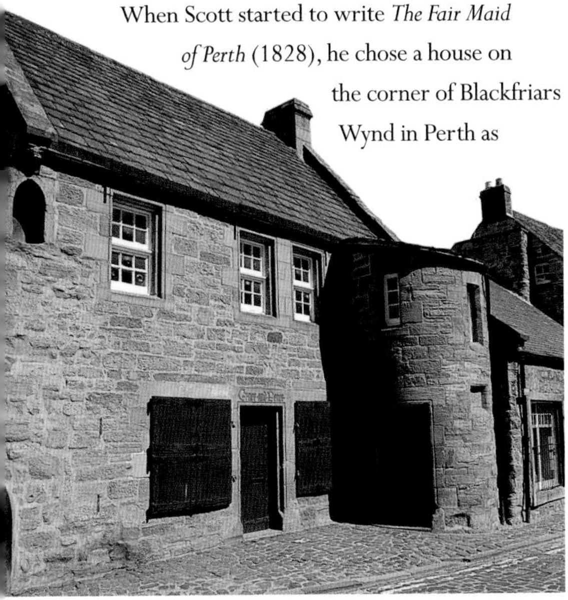

◀ *Sir Walter Scott chose Fair Maid's House in Perth as the home of Catherine Glover, the heroine of* The Fair Maid of Perth *(1828).*

ⓘ information

Contact details

Fair Maid's House
North Port
Perth
Perthshire, PH1 5LU

🌐 Royal Scottish Geographical Society:
www.rsgs.org/projects/fmh.html

Transport links

🚆 Perth

🚗 A989 circles Perth and the M90 is nearby

BIRNAM WOOD
PERTHSHIRE

See map p. 135 **11**

KEY FIGURES:	William Shakespeare; Beatrix Potter
KEY LOCATIONS:	Birnam Oak; Dalguise House; Birnam; Dunkeld

An ancient tree called the Birnam Oak stands behind the Birnam House Hotel. It is believed to be the last survivor of Birnam Wood, which was immortalized by William Shakespeare in *Macbeth* (shown below). In the play, the three witches warn Macbeth that his days will be numbered when the wood starts to move. This happens when the army of his enemy, Malcolm, cuts branches from the trees in the wood and, while holding them, stealthily advances towards Macbeth's troops. The ensuing battle takes place on Dunsinane Hill, about 15 miles away – which casts doubt over the authenticity of the Birnam Oak.

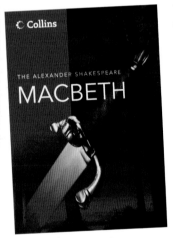

Each summer while Beatrix Potter was in her teens, the Potter family rented Dalguise House, near Birnam. She loved the countryside, and later wrote 'I remember every stone, every tree, the scent of the heather.' She became friendly with the local naturalist, Charles Macintosh, who encouraged her to draw what she found. In 1893, while staying in nearby Dunkeld, Beatrix wrote an illustrated story-letter to the son of her former governess, which formed the basis of what later became *The Tale of Peter Rabbit* (1902). She was 27 when she wrote the letter and 36 when *Peter Rabbit* was published. Beatrix used the name of her own pet rabbit, Peter, who went everywhere with her on his lead.

Beatrix Potter's connections with Birnam are remembered in the exhibition mounted by the Birnam Institute and in the Beatrix Potter Garden, which recreates many of the characters from her books.

ⓘ information

Contact details
Birnam
Dunkeld
Perth and Kinross

Perthshire Guide:
www.perthshire.co.uk

Transport links
Dunkeld and Birnam

The A9 passes through Birnam

THE FALLS OF MONESS

PERTHSHIRE

See map p.135 **12**

KEY FIGURE: Robert Burns
KEY LOCATION: Birks of Aberfeldy

On 30 August 1787 Robert Burns took one of his favourite walks up the Birks of Aberfeldy. He stopped a short way up the birks and sat on a stone ledge to watch the water from the Falls of Moness tumbling past. The experience inspired him to write a song, called 'The Birks of Aberfeldy'. The birks was named for the birch trees that grow here and is a woodland walk that runs through a valley near Aberfeldy. The 'crystal streamlet' is the Moness Burn, which is a tributary of the River Tay. The entire walk, including the stone on which Burns sat – now called Burns' Seat – is clearly marked.

Burns was starting to make a name for himself at the time of his walk, having published his first volume of poetry, *Poems, Chiefly in the Scottish Dialect*, in 1786. In May 1787, he embarked on what he called 'a slight pilgrimage to the classic

▲ *The Falls of Moness inspired Robert Burns to write his classic song 'The Birks of Aberfeldy'.*

scenes of this country [Scotland]', and it was during this trip that he visited the Falls of Moness.

(i) information

Contact details

Birks of Aberfeldy
Aberfeldy
Perth and Kinross
PH15 2DD

🖥 Perthshire Information:
www.perthshire.co.uk

☎ Tourist Information:
+44 (0)1887 820276

Transport links

🚆 Pitlochry

🚗 The A827 and A826 run through Aberfeldy

BARRIE'S BIRTHPLACE
ANGUS

See map p.135 (13)

KEY FIGURE: James Barrie
KEY LOCATION: Kirriemuir

On 9 May 1860, James Barrie was born at 9 Brechin Road, Kirriemuir. It was a modest, white-washed cottage and the Barries were a working-class family – his father was a handloom-weaver. Barrie was the ninth of 10 children, and in later years he claimed that his birth coincided with the arrival of some new dining room chairs, which apparently gave his parents more pleasure than his entrance into the world.

Kirriemuir strongly influenced Barrie's later writing. In the 1880s, he wrote a series of novels set in a town called Thrums (a weaving term), which was Kirriemuir under another name. The wash-house at the back of the home was the model for the house in *Peter Pan* (1904) that the Lost Boys built for Wendy in Never-Never Land.

The house next door to Barrie's birthplace is now a museum dedicated to the life of the author.

▲ *James Barrie chose to be buried in the local Kirriemuir cemetery rather than Westminster Abbey.*

In 2010, new artefacts were added to the museum including a manuscript of *Peter Pan* and the Barrie family christening gown.

(i) information

Contact details

J M Barrie's Birthplace
9 Brechin Road
Kirriemuir, Angus
DD8 4BX

☎ +44 (0)844 493 2142

National Trust:
www.nts.org.uk/Property/37

Transport links

Dundee (15 miles)

The A928 and B957
run through Kirriemuir

ARBUTHNOTT
ABERDEENSHIRE

See map p. 135 (14)

KEY FIGURE: James Leslie Mitchell
KEY LOCATIONS: Bloomfield; The Grassic Gibbon Centre

It was while living in Arbuthnott that James Leslie Mitchell (1901–35) wrote his trilogy of novels, collectively called *A Scots Quair* (1946), under the pen name of Lewis Grassic Gibbon. *Sunset Song* (1932), *Cloud Howe* (1933) and *Grey Granite* (1934) told the story of Chris Guthrie, who grew up on her father's farm, was married three times and whose son joined the Communist Party. The novels were rich in Scots dialect and ancient Scots phrases, and celebrated Mitchell's love for his native land.

Mitchell was born at Hillhead of Seggat, where he lived with his crofting family until they moved to Bloomfield in Arbuthnott, in the countryside known as Howe of the Mearns. He later went to Aberdeen and Glasgow, where he worked as a journalist, and then lived in the south of England with his wife. In 1929, he became

▲ *The Grassic Gibbon Centre, near Arbuthnott Parish Hall, celebrates the life of James Leslie Mitchell.*

a professional writer and wrote 17 books in 7 years. Also under his pseudonym, he wrote *Scottish Scene* (1934), the collection of short stories on which he and the poet, Hugh MacDiarmid, collaborated.

ⓘ information

Contact details

Arbuthnott
Laurencekirk
Aberdeenshire
AB30

☎ +44 (0)1224 288828

🖳 Local Council:
www.aberdeenshire.gov.uk/visit/index.asp

The Grassic Gibbon Centre:
www.grassicgibbon.com

Transport links

🚆 Stonehaven

🚗 The B967 runs through Arbuthnott

SANDAIG
HIGHLAND

See map p. 135 **15**

KEY FIGURE: Gavin Maxwell
KEY LOCATIONS: Sandaig; Eilean Ban

This is Gavin Maxwell's (1914–69) Camusfeàrna, where he lived with his otters, Edal, Mijbil and Teko, in a lighthouse keeper's cottage at the edge of the Sound of Sleat. Maxwell came here after a failed attempt at shark-fishing on Soay off Skye, which he wrote about in his first book, *Harpoon at a Venture* (1952). Sandaig offered the simple life that Maxwell craved, although it changed forever after he wrote about it in *Ring of Bright Water* (1960). Maxwell called the place Camusfeàrna rather than by its real name because, he said, such places should remain in the reader's imagination.

Maxwell's house burnt down in 1968, and his favourite otter, Edal, died in the fire. Maxwell died a year later and his grave is marked by a large boulder placed where his desk once stood.

In 1963, Maxwell had bought three cottages on Eilean Bàn, a tiny island in the Sound of Sleat, but he did not move to the island until 1968.

▲ *Gavin Maxwell's desk and the tools he used for observing otters are on display in the Long Room.*

His home there is now called the Long Room and can be visited, whereas the island has become a commemorative otter sanctuary. The Bright Water Visitor Centre, which is dedicated to Maxwell's work, is at Kyleakin on Skye.

(i) information

Contact details
Sandaig
Glenelg
Kyle

www Travel Information:
www.what-sthere.co.uk/
sandaig.htm

Transport links
Kyle of Lochalsh

The A87 runs nearby

ISLE OF SKYE
HIGHLAND

See map p.135 (16)

KEY FIGURE: Mary Stewart; Dr Samuel Johnson; James Boswell; Sorley MacLean
KEY LOCATIONS: Cuillin Hills; Dunvegan Castle; Portree; Kingsburgh

Mary Stewart (born 1916), who has written many popular suspense novels and thrillers, chose the Isle of Skye as the setting for her novel *Wildfire at Midnight* (1956). In it she conjured up the strange atmosphere of the Cuillin Hills. The heroine, Gianetta, is battling with a nervous breakdown when she takes a holiday on Skye, but rather than the relaxation she was hoping for she has to cope with a killer on the loose and the disturbing presence of her ex-husband.

Life was less eventful for Dr Samuel Johnson and James Boswell when they visited Skye during their tour of Scotland in 1773. They stayed on the island for a month, during which time they enjoyed plenty of Scottish hospitality and stayed in some of the best houses. They spent 10 days at Dunvegan Castle, where Johnson enjoyed the food immeasurably. When they visited Portree, they dined at McNab's and believed it to be the only inn on the island. One of the most memorable parts of their stay was meeting Flora Macdonald at Kingsburgh. She gave them a first-hand account of helping Bonnie Prince Charlie to escape to France in 1746, for which she was briefly imprisoned in the Tower of London.

Just after the end of the First World War, a young Sorley MacLean used to catch the ferry from his home on the Isle of Raasay to go to school at Portree on Skye. After training to be a teacher at Edinburgh University and stints as a teacher on Ross and the Isle of Mull, he returned to teach on Skye. He remained a teacher all his working life, writing poetry in his spare time.

A more recent resident on the island is the Scots poet Kevin MacNeil, who was the inaugural writer in residence for the Highland area of Scotland. His work includes *Love and Zen in the Outer Hebrides* (1998) and *BeWise Be Otherwise* (2001).

(i) information

Contact details
Isle of Skye
Highlands

Local Information:
www.skye.co.uk

Transport links
Kyle of Lochalsh

The A87 runs nearby

SLAINS CASTLE

ABERDEENSHIRE

See map p. 135 (17)

KEY FIGURES: Dr Samuel Johnson; James Boswell; Bram Stoker
KEY LOCATIONS: Slains Castle; Cruden Bay

Although Slains Castle (shown below) is now a ruin looking out to sea near Cruden Bay, it was once a perfectly habitable home. In 1773, Dr Samuel Johnson and his faithful friend and later biographer, James Boswell, visited the castle and stayed with the Earl and Countess of Errol who then owned it. Both men were on a tour of Scotland, which Johnson wrote about in his *A Journey to the Western Islands of Scotland* (1775). Boswell recorded his own impressions in *Journal of a Tour to the Hebrides* (1785), which was published a year after Johnson's death. In it, Boswell noted that the walls of one of the towers at Slains seemed to extend directly from the rock on which the castle perched.

In the 1890s, Bram Stoker enjoyed his journeys to this part of Scotland. The craggy scenery fired his imagination and Slains Castle made a particular impression on him. His story, 'Mystery of the Sea', was based on a local ghost story. He started writing *Dracula*, in 1895, and it seems that he had Slains Castle in mind when he wrote about Dracula's castle in Transylvania. There is even evidence that in an early draft of the novel Dracula came ashore at Cruden Bay rather than at Whitby, as in the final version (see page 131).

(i) information

Contact details

Slains Castle
near Cruden Bay
Peterhead
Aberdeenshire AB42

Online Guide:
www.undiscoveredscotland.co.
uk/crudenbay/slainscastle

Transport links

Aberdeen

The A93, A956, A975 and
A9013 run through Aberdeen

MUCKLE FLUGGA
SHETLAND ISLANDS

See map p. 135 **18**

KEY FIGURE: Robert Louis Stevenson
KEY LOCATION: Unst

Robert Louis Stevenson was born into a celebrated family of engineers; his father, Thomas, designed many of the lighthouses that ring the coast of Scotland. Although the young Robert began to study engineering at Edinburgh University he soon had to tell his father that he would not be following in his footsteps, and instead he turned to the law before finally satisfying his urge to become a writer.

Stevenson frequently accompanied his father on his trips to the lighthouses that were being built under his instructions, and in 1869 they went to Muckle Flugga, on Unst, to see a lighthouse that was commissioned to help protect ships during the Crimean war. It is the most northerly lighthouse in Britain and stands in a dramatic and atmospheric setting, perched on the top of jagged rocks at the northern head of Unst.

▲ *Robert Louis Stevenson's* Treasure Island *recalls the landscape of Muckle Flugga, which he visited in 1869.*

The island made a big impact on Stevenson and he must have stored his memories of it at the back of his mind because when he came to write *Treasure Island* 14 years later, the map of the island bore a remarkable resemblance to that of Unst.

 **information**

Contact details
Muckle Flugga
Unst
Shetland Islands

💻 Northern Lighthouse Board:
www.nlb.org.uk

Transport links
⛴ Belmont (Unst Shetland)
Gutcher Shetland

The A968 runs through Unst

WALES

Wales may only be a small nation, but it has an enormous literary heritage that stretches across many writing genres. Roald Dahl was born and grew up in Cardiff, where he experienced a world of dictatorial grown-ups and greedy schoolchildren that he wrote about in his well-loved children's stories. Some Welsh writers have become so famous that it seems as though the entire culture of their country rests on their shoulders. One of these is Dylan Thomas, who packed an incredible amount of living, drinking and writing into his relatively short life. R.S. Thomas chose to live a very different sort of life on Llyn Peninsula. Robert Graves found in Harlech the tranquility and freedom that was missing from his life in London, whereas Percy Bysshe Shelley encountered anything but peace during his time in Tremadog.

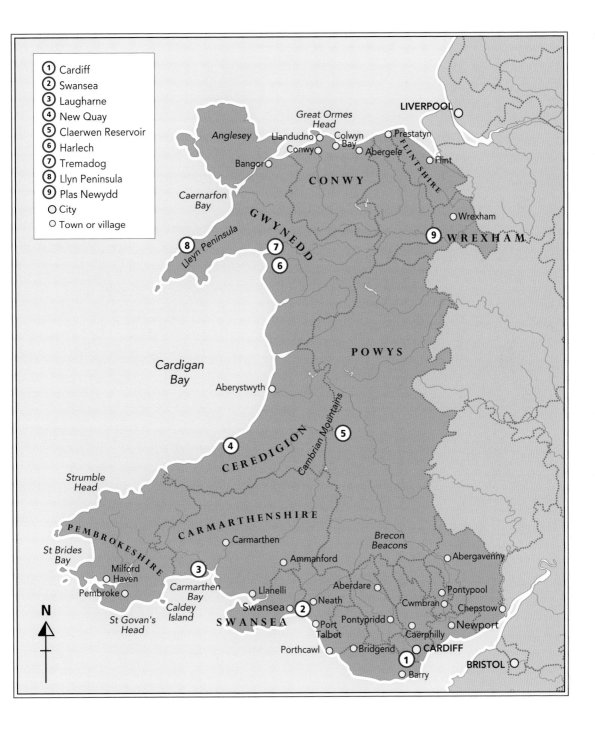

1 Cardiff
2 Swansea
3 Laugharne
4 New Quay
5 Claerwen Reservoir
6 Harlech
7 Tremadog
8 Llyn Peninsula
9 Plas Newydd
○ City
○ Town or village

LIVERPOOL

Great Ormes
Head

Anglesey
Llandudno
Conwy
Colwyn
Bay
Abergele
Prestatyn
Flint

Bangor

CONWY

FLINTSHIRE

Wrexham

Caernarfon
Bay

GWYNEDD

8 Lleyn Peninsula

7

6

9 WREXHAM

POWYS

Cardigan
Bay

Aberystwyth

Cambrian Mountains

5

4

CEREDIGION

Strumble
Head

PEMBROKESHIRE

CARMARTHENSHIRE

Brecon
Beacons

Abergavenny

St Brides
Bay

Milford
Haven

Pembroke

3

Carmarthen

Ammanford

Aberdare

Pontypool

Cwmbran

Chepstow

Carmarthen
Bay
Caldey
Island

Llanelli

Swansea

2

Neath

SWANSEA

Port
Talbot

Pontypridd

Caerphilly

Newport

St Govan's
Head

N

Porthcawl

Bridgend

1 CARDIFF

BRISTOL

Barry

CARDIFF

KEY FIGURE:	Roald Dahl
KEY LOCATIONS:	Norwegian Seamen's Church; Roald Dahl Plass

The writing career of Roald Dahl (1916–90) effectively began during the Second World War when he fractured his skull in an aeroplane crash. During his recovery he had some strange dreams, which he wrote down. He wrote *The Gremlins* in 1943, followed by a book of short stories about his exploits in the RAF called *Over to You* (1946). More short stories followed and in 1961 *James and the Giant Peach* was published in America (it did not appear in Britain for another six years), marking the start

▲ *Johnny Depp stars as the eccentric Willy Wonka in Tim Burton's 2005 film version of Roald Dahl's classic.*

of Dahl's career as the author of children's books, in which he created a world where children got their own back on dictatorial adults.

Dahl was born to Norwegian parents in Cardiff's leafy suburb of Llandaff in 1916. His early childhood was very happy, but his father and elder sister both died when Roald was three and his mother had to sell her jewellery to pay for his education, first at Llandaff Cathedral School and later at Repton in Derbyshire.

Roald and his sisters were christened in the Norwegian Seamen's Church in Cardiff Docks. The church was derelict by the 1980s, and Roald Dahl was the first president of the trust that was set up to restore it, although he died in 1990 before the restoration was complete.

In 2002, the Oval Basin in Cardiff Docks changed its name to Roald Dahl Plass, in honour of his Norwegian ancestry.

ⓘ information

Contact details

Cardiff

 Tourist Information:
+44 (0)29 2087 3573

 Tourist Information:
www.visitcardiff.com

Transport links

 Cardiff Central

The M4 runs along Cardiff, and A48 runs through

SWANSEA
SWANSEA

See map p.163 ②

KEY FIGURES: Dylan Thomas; Kingsley Amis
KEY LOCATIONS: Dylan Thomas Centre; Cwmdonkin Drive; Bryn-y-Mor pub

---

'Land of my fathers. My fathers can keep it.' So said Dylan Thomas (shown right), one of Wales's most famous poets, whose memory is kept alive in his hometown at the Dylan Thomas Centre. Thomas was born in Swansea on 27 October 1914, at 5 Cwmdonkin Drive in the Uplands part of the city.

In 1925, Thomas went to Swansea Grammar School and in 1931 he became a junior reporter on the *South Wales Daily Post*. Thomas moved to London in 1934 and continued to work as a journalist, as well as branching out into film-making and broadcasting. He quickly became known as a heavy drinker, propping up the bars of Soho and, in the 1950s, of New York.

Swansea was the home of another man who liked a drink. This was Kingsley Amis, who spent 12 years as a lecturer in English literature at Swansea University from 1949. After starting off in a poky flat, Kingsley and Hilly Amis, and their two sons Philip and Martin, moved to a house very close to Dylan Thomas's old home in Cwmdonkin Drive. It was here that Kingsley Amis launched his writing career with *Lucky Jim* (1954). Amis described his experiences in Swansea in his *Memoirs* (1991), including his encounters with Dylan Thomas, who he described as 'an outstandingly unpleasant man', and his wife, Caitlin (1913–94), as well as with Thomas's last mistress, Elizabeth Reitell. Amis used to drink at the Bryn-y-Mor pub and, long after he had moved away, he retained a strong affection for the city.

ⓘ information

Contact details

Swansea
Neath Port Talbot

☎ Tourist Information:
+44 (0)1792 468321

🖳 Tourist Information:
www.visitswanseabay.com

Transport links

🚃 Swansea

🚗 The A483 and A4067 run through Swansea, the M4 is nearby

LAUGHARNE
CARMARTHENSHIRE

See map p.163 ③

KEY FIGURE: Dylan Thomas
KEY LOCATIONS: The Boathouse; St Martin's Church

When Dylan Thomas fell in love with Caitlin Macnamara in the summer of 1936, he also fell in love with Laugharne, the setting of the romance.

Thomas and Caitlin married in 1937 and moved to Laugharne in 1938. They moved from house to house, but in 1940 the couple and their first child, Llewelyn, fled Laugharne to escape their debts.

In 1949 the couple moved back to Laugharne to The Boathouse. By now, Thomas was a renowned poet, and in 1950 he left Wales for his first tour of the United States. Although he was still writing, his drinking and private life – Dylan had started an affair at this point – were distracting.

In the summer of 1951, he completed the first half of his most famous work, *Under Milk Wood*. This recorded 24 hours in the town of Llareggub, which was Laugharne by another name and which, when spelt backwards, described Thomas's changed feelings for the place.

▲ *The Boathouse, where Dylan Thomas worked in the last four years of his life, is now open to the public.*

While in New York in November 1935, Thomas collapsed and died from complications brought on by his heavy drinking. His body was brought back to Laugharne and buried in St Martin's churchyard, his grave marked by a simple white cross. He was only 39 years old.

ⓘ information

Contact details

Laugharne
Carmarthen
Dyfed

 Tourist Information:
www.walesdirectory.co.uk/
Towns_in_Wales/Laugharne
_Town.htm

Transport links

 Ferryside

The A4066 runs through Laugharne

NEW QUAY
PEMBROKESHIRE

See map p.163 (4)

KEY FIGURE:	Dylan Thomas
KEY LOCATIONS:	Black Lion pub; Fishguard

Dylan Thomas knew this stretch of the Pembrokeshire coast well and was friends with Jack Patrick, the publican of the Black Lion pub in New Quay. There was nothing unusual about Thomas having friends in the pub trade, as he conducted a life-long love affair with alcohol, even though it did him no good at all and eventually killed him. It also distracted him from his work, and his wife, Caitlin, complained that he became 'Instant Dylan' whenever he was drunkenly entertaining his friends in bars.

Thomas was a prolific poet in his youth, concentrating almost three-quarters of his work into a three-year period during the 1930s. In the early 1950s, towards the end of what turned out to be a very short life, he began to experiment with prose, and described the walk along the cliffs of New Quay in *Quite Early One Morning*, which was published posthumously in 1954.

▲ *The* Under Milk Wood *(1953) and* Moby Dick *(1851) films were shot in Fishguard in 1971 and 1955 respectively.*

A few miles down the coast, to the southwest, is the idyllic town of Fishguard. The Lower Town hugs the harbour and is where the film of *Under Milk Wood*, one of Thomas's best-known works, which he finished shortly before his death, was filmed in 1971.

(i) information

Contact details

New Quay
Ceredigion
Dyfed

 Tourist Information: www.tourism.ceredigion. gov.uk/saesneg/newquay.htm

Transport links

Fishguard Harbour

 The A486 runs through New Quay

CLAERWEN RESERVOIR

POWYS

See map p.163 ⑤

KEY FIGURES: Percy Bysshe Shelley; T.J. Hogg; Francis Brett Young
KEY LOCATIONS: Claerwen Reservoir; Caban Coch Reservoir

In March 1811, Percy Bysshe Shelley (1792–1822) and his friend T.J. Hogg (1792–1862) were expelled from Oxford for writing and circulating a pamphlet with the inflammatory title *The Necessity of Atheism*. Shelley visited his cousin, Thomas Grove, who lived at Cwm Elan, a house that lies below the Claerwen Reservoir. His young guest found it 'gloomy and desolate', but, despite this, he returned in April 1812 with his young wife, Harriet. They stayed at NantGwyllt, a house on the west shore of Caban Coch, on the road to the Claerwen Reservoir, until June 1812 when they moved on again. Water played a prominent part in their lives and in their deaths: Harriet drowned herself in the Serpentine in London's Hyde Park in 1816, and Shelley drowned in a boating accident in Italy in 1822.

The Elan Valley, to which the Claerwen and Caban Coch Reservoirs belong, was part of the

▲ *Percy Bysshe Shelley's radical pamphleteering aggravated the British government.*

landscape in many of the novels of Francis Brett Young (1884–1954). His childhood memories of spending time at the reservoirs inspired his novels, which include *The House Under the Water* (1932).

ⓘ information

Contact details

Claerwen Reservoir
Ystrad Fflur
Powys

Transport links

 Llanwrtyd (12 miles)
Garth (Powys) (12 miles)

 The A470 is nearby

HARLECH
GWYNEDD

See map p. 163 ⑥

KEY FIGURE: Robert Graves
KEY LOCATION: Harlech Castle

As a small boy, Robert Graves (1895–1985) accompanied his family on their summer trips to Harlech. He grew up in London and had little feeling for the city. Homelife in the Graves household was rigorously structured, running by strict Victorian standards. Graves's father was A.P. Graves (1846–1931), an Irish bard who used to attend the Eisteddfod in Wales and who helped to establish the Welsh Folk Song Society. His mother, Amalie, was deeply religious with an almost compulsive sense of right and wrong, which she taught Robert. His schooldays were troubled – he was frightened of displeasing his mother and he attended a total of seven schools.

Harlech and Wales offered the freedom he lacked in the city. Robert and his sister, Rosaleen, would roam around the hills behind Harlech and, encouraged by their father, they collected the Welsh folk songs sung by the local inhabitants and recorded them on the phonograph they carried with them. Graves was terrified of heights and he felt compelled to face his fears in the castle, where he'd hide in the ruined walls and force himself to look down. Graves was in Harlech on holiday in August 1914 when war was declared on Germany. He immediately enlisted and was given a commission in the Royal Welch Fusiliers. When Graves moved to Majorca in 1929, he chose a place with scenery that was as close to that of Harlech as he could find. This was the year when his autobiography, *Goodbye to All That*, was published. Its matter-of-fact descriptions of the horrors of life in the trenches on the Western Front sent shock waves through Britain.

Graves was entranced by the magic of Wales and, in addition to his poetry, he wrote several books about mythology including *The White Goddess* (1948) and *The Greek Myths* (1955).

(i) information

Contact details

Harlech
Snowdonia National Park
Gwynedd
LL46 2

www Tourist Information:
www.harlech.com/harlech.html

Transport links

🚉 Harlech

🚗 The A496 runs by Harlech

TREMADOG
GWYNEDD

See map p.163 ⑦

KEY FIGURES: Percy Bysshe Shelley; T.E. Lawrence
KEY LOCATIONS: Tan-yr-Allt; Woodlands

The village of Tremadog was designed and built by W. A. Madocks, who planned to build, among other things, a causeway that would reclaim some of the land in the Glaslyn estuary. The poet Percy Bysshe Shelley thought it was such a good idea that he offered to help him raise funds.

In September 1812, Shelley and his 17-year-old wife, Harriet, moved into a house, which has since been demolished, on Madocks's Tan-yr-Allt estate. Here, Shelley wrote a large part of *Queen Mab* (1813), a polemic in which he advocates free love, atheism and vegetarianism among other ideas. The vegetarianism in particular caused problems with the local shepherds. Matters finally came to a head in February 1813 when intruders burst into the house and fired shots. He and Harriet left as soon as possible afterwards.

T.E. Lawrence, who also excited comment, was born at Woodlands in Tremadog in 1888.

▲ *Percy Bysshe Shelley annoyed farmers by killing sick or injured sheep while walking through Tremadog.*

ⓘ information

Contact details

Tremadog
Porthmadog
Gwynedd

Historical Information:
www.tremadog.org.uk

Transport links

Porthmadog

The A487 runs through
Porthmadog

LLYN PENINSULA
GWYNEDD

See map p. 163 (8)

KEY FIGURES: R.S. Thomas; Jan Morris
KEY LOCATIONS: Manafon; Pentrefelin; Llanystumdwy

R.S. Thomas (1913–2000) was a poet and priest who spent his life championing the Welsh cause. He spoke out against what he saw as the horrors of contemporary life, such as its 'awful atheism' and the 'cultural suicide' that was being practised in Wales. Thomas was never afraid to speak his mind, even if his views resulted in controversy.

He was born in Cardiff, but his family moved to Holyhead on the Isle of Anglesey when he was five. At first, Thomas spoke only English, but he made a point of learning and speaking Welsh. His autobiography, *Neb*, was written in Welsh in 1985 and was later translated into English, although not by him, and published as *Autobiographies* (1997).

Thomas was a priest of the Church of Wales, and his strong belief in God informed his poetry. He wrote most of the poems in his first three collections of poetry while he was the rector of Manafon, near Welshpool. His poem, 'The Other', is inscribed on slate in the church of St Hywyn, Aberdaron, where he was the priest for 11 years. After spending 40 years as a parish priest, Thomas retired to a stone cottage at Pentrefelin, near Criccieth, where the views of Llyn Peninsula inspired his work and fuelled his belief that Wales should retain its own cultural identity. He died there in 2000.

Jan Morris (born 1926) is another famed author who is strongly associated with Llyn. She is a celebrated travel writer who has written about many of the greatest cities in the world, including New York in *The Great Port* (1969) and *Venice* (1960), but who always returns home to the village of Llanystumdwy, near Criccieth, where she has lived for over 30 years. Jan wrote about her Welsh home, Trefan Morys, and about Wales – literally the land of her father, as he was Welsh – in *A Writer's House in Wales* (2001).

ⓘ information

Contact details

Llyn Peninsula
Llanbedrog
Gwynedd

🌐 Local Information:
www.llyn.info

Transport links

🚆 Pwllheli

🚗 The A499 and A497 run through Lynn Peninsula

PLAS NEWYDD
DENBIGHSHIRE

See map p. 163 (9)

KEY FIGURES: Lady Eleanor Butler; Hon. Sarah Ponsonby
KEY LOCATION: Plas Newydd; St Collen Church

This is the house of the 'Ladies of Llangollen', two Irish spinsters from aristocratic families who caused a sensation when they eloped to Britain together in 1778. They had been close friends – no one knows how close, although there has been much speculation about the precise nature of their relationship – for 10 years when they decided to escape from their families across the Irish Sea, dressed in men's clothing and with only one faithful servant, Mary Caryll, to help them. At the time, Lady Eleanor Butler was 39 and the Hon. Sarah Ponsonby was 23. Their families intervened, but the women eventually managed to reach Britain, and the entire episode became the talk of Georgian society.

Eleanor and Sarah came to live at a cottage called Pen-y-Maes, which they renamed Plas

Newydd ('New Place'; shown opposite). Now that the sisters were estranged from their families, they had to adjust to a more frugal lifestyle but this didn't stop them transforming the house into a temple to Gothic architecture. They searched old churches for oak carvings and stained glass windows and their friends brought them gifts to decorate their home. The women spent almost 50 years here, during which time they prided themselves on improving their minds through culture and read the work of such people as the French philosopher Jean-Jacques Rousseau (1712–78) aloud to one another. As a result, they became a magnet for the many literary celebrities of their day, such as Sir Walter Scott, Robert Southey, Percy Bysshe Shelley, Lord Byron and William Wordsworth, who gave the women a particularly beautiful oak chair.

Eleanor died in 1829 and Sarah died two years later, and their house is now open to the public. Their letters, which they always signed jointly, and journals are now considered to be so important that they are held at the National Library of Wales. The women were buried in the churchyard of St Collen in Llangollen.

▲ The 'Ladies of Llangollen' gained celebrity status and were granted a civil list pension by Queen Charlotte.

(i) information

Contact details

Plas Newydd
Mill Street
Llangollen
Denbighshire

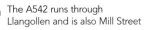 Derbyshire County Council:
www.denbighshire.gov.
uk/en-gb/DNAP-73FFMH

☎ +44 (0)1978 862834

Transport links

🚆 Chirk

🚗 The A542 runs through
Llangollen and is also Mill Street

NORTHERN IRELAND AND IRELAND

Northern Ireland has had more than its fair share of difficulties, especially with the sectarian violence of the 20th century. Many writers born in Northern Ireland moved over the border to the Republic as soon as they were able, or made for America instead where they were justifiably fêted. Nevertheless, there are some towering names connected with Northern Ireland, including those of Seamus Heaney, Brian Friel and C.S. Lewis. Thoughts of the Republic of Ireland conjure up images of beautiful countryside, sparkling bays and a more gentle way of life. Dublin is one of the most beautiful cities in the world and is also steeped in literary connections. Who can forget that this is where James Joyce was born and lived until moving to Europe? This is the country of J.M. Synge, Lady Gregory, Samuel Beckett and Patrick Kavanagh, of poets, playwrights, novelists and critics.

Map Legend

1. Strabane
2. Kilclogher
3. Belfast
4. The Brontë Homeland
5. Inniskeen
6. Coole Park Nature Reserve
7. Synge's Cottage
8. Howth
9. Dublin

a. The James Joyce Centre
b. Abbey Theatre
c. Trinity College
d. St Patrick's Cathedral

○ City
○ Town or village
■■■ International border

ATLANTIC OCEAN

UNITED KINGDOM →

Tory Island
Malin Head
Rathlin Island
Coleraine
LONDONDERRY
NORTHERN IRELAND
DONEGAL
Larne
GALWAY
ANTRIM
Carrickfergus
Cookstown
Bangor
TYRONE
BELFAST
Sligo
Portadown
Armagh
DOWN
SLIGO
Newry
Dundrum Bay
Cavan
Dundalk
CAVAN
LOUTH
LONGFORD
Drogheda
Navan
MEATH
Athlone
N
Galway
GALWAY
OFFALY
Aran Islands
DUBLIN (see inset)
Bray
REPUBLIC OF IRELAND
KILDARE
Portlaoise
IRISH SEA
LAOIS
WICKLOW
Loop Head
LIMERICK
LIMERICK
KILKENNY
Tipperary
Clonmel
WATERFORD
WATERFORD
KERRY
CORK
CORK
Mizen Head
Old Head of Kinsale
St George's Channel
CELTIC SEA

DUBLIN inset

DUBLIN
Cumberland St
Constitution Hill
Dorset St
Parnell St
Connolly Station
O'Connell St
Bolton St
Capel St
Bolton St
River Liffey
Inns Quay
Merchants Qy
Wellington Qy
Aston Qy
Townsend St
Dame St
Pearse Street
Nassau St
Pearse Station
Dame St
Grafton St
The Coombe
St Georges St
Aungier St
Wexford St
North
South
Nicholas St
Harcourt St
Harrington St
Adelaide Rd

STRABANE
COUNTY TYRONE

See map p.175 (1)

KEY FIGURE:	Flann O'Brien
KEY LOCATION:	Bowling Green

Many people, when asked to name an Irish comic writer, immediately think of Flann O'Brien (1911–66), whose surreal flights of fancy continue to amuse readers. Brian O Nuallain, to give him his real name, was born at 15 Bowling Green, Strabane. His family were Gaelic-speaking and were determined that the young Brian should not mix with anyone who spoke English. However, O'Brien began to speak English after overhearing the forbidden tongue being spoken.

The family moved to Dublin where O'Brien attended the city's University College. In a ghastly ironic twist, his father died from a stroke on the same day in July 1937 that O'Brien had passed his exams and been accepted into the civil service, and he found himself having to work to support his mother and 10 siblings. It was around this time that he began to write his first novel,

At Swim-Two-Birds (1939), which concerned a novelist called Dermot Trellis, who was in turn being written about by his own characters. The book was championed by James Joyce (1882–1941) and Graham Greene, among others, but this was no help when it came to getting O'Brien's next novel, *The Third Policeman*, published. After suffering rejection after rejection from publishers in 1939, O'Brien put it to one side and let it gather dust for the rest of his life.

In 1953, O'Brien was asked to leave the civil service partly because of his growing alcoholism and because of a column he wrote in the *The Irish Times*, which broke civil service rules by making political statements in public. These columns appeared in book form after O'Brien's death in 1966, as did *The Third Policeman*. This novel has been celebrated as a classic piece of writing ever since.

(i) information

Contact details

Strabane
County Tyrone
BT82

☎ +44 (0)28 7138 2204

[www] Strabane District Council:
www.strabanedc.com

Transport links

🚆 Londonderry (13 miles)

🚗 The N14 and the A5 run through Strabane

KILLYCLOGHER
COUNTY TYRONE

See map p.175 (2)

KEY FIGURE: Brian Friel
KEY LOCATION: Killyclogher

When Brian Friel (born 1929) was born in Killyclogher (shown below) near Omagh, he entered what he later described as 'inbred claustrophobic Ireland'. The country was in the grip of massive political changes and upheavals, all of which influenced Friel when he began his career as a writer. He was also aware of deep divisions within his own family – his grandparents came from County Donegal, were illiterate and only spoke Irish, whereas their son was a teacher. The contrasts between modern Ulster and traditional Ireland are a recurring theme in Friel's work.

The young Brian went to Long Tower School in Derry, where his father taught, and later attended St Columb's College. He trained to be a teacher at St Joseph's Training College in Belfast, working in the city until 1960. At this point, Friel abandoned his teaching career in order to become a full-time writer of plays and short stories.

It has been an illustrious career, and Friel is one of the best-known writers in Ireland. His plays, which include *Philadelphia, Here I Come!* (1964) and *Dancing at Lughnasa* (1990), have been particularly successful.

(i) information

Contact details
Killyclogher
Omagh
BT79

Transport links
 The A505 runs by Killyclogher

BELFAST
NORTHERN IRELAND

See map p. 175 ③

KEY FIGURES: C.S. Lewis; Samuel Beckett; Seamus Heaney
KEY LOCATIONS: Holywood Road Branch Library; Linen Hall Library; Campbell College

The capital city of Northern Ireland, Belfast was once a city that thrived on shipbuilding and the cloth trade. However, when the Troubles flared up in the 1960s it became notorious for bitter and bloody sectarian divisions between Catholics and Protestants. That has changed since the ceasefire of 1994 and the beleaguered city is now rebuilding itself.

Strangely, in a country that prides itself on its rich and influential literary heritage, there are very few monuments to Irish writers in Belfast. One of these rarities is the life-sized statue of C.S. Lewis (1898–1963) outside the Holywood Road Branch Library. It shows him opening the door of a wardrobe, in homage to his world-famous Narnia Chronicles, which began with *The Lion, the Witch and the Wardrobe* in 1950 (shown left). The Linen Hall Library has a collection of books that are either by or about Lewis.

The Lion, the Witch and the Wardrobe
C. S. LEWIS

The Chronicles of Narnia
FULL-COLOUR COLLECTOR'S EDITION

Seamus Heaney's Mossbawn

Mossbawn is the name of the cattle farm in Tamniarn, Londonderry, where Seamus Heaney was born. He was the eldest of nine children who went on to become one of Ireland's greatest contemporary poets.

Heaney's poems show that he has never forgotten growing up in Londonderry. He wrote vividly of his childhood home in North (1975) in which two of the poems are entitled 'Mossbawn'. His mother, Margaret, died in 1984 and The Haw Lantern (1987) contains a sequence of sonnets about her. His father, Patrick, died soon after and was remembered in many of the poems in Seeing Things (1991).

Heaney's childhood home has not forgotten him, either. There is an exhibition devoted to him at Bellaghy Bawn, the Plantation castle at Bellaghy, including a film of him talking about the impact that the area has had on his poetry.

Clive Staples Lewis was born in Strandtown, Belfast, in 1898 and grew up here. He was a strong-minded boy who decided at the age of four that he would henceforth be known as Jacksie – this was shortened to Jacks and finally

▲ *The statue of C.S. Lewis in east Belfast was erected in 1998 to mark the centenary of the author's birth.*

to Jack. He wrote about his Belfast childhood, including his short spell as a boarder at Campbell College in 1910, in *Surprised by Joy* (1955).

In 1928, the playwright Samuel Beckett (1906–89) spent two terms teaching French at Campbell College before moving to Paris, where he met James Joyce (1882–1941) and became his secretary. Belfast has always prided itself on its education and its students include Tom Paulin (born 1949), the poet, playwright and critic, who went to Annadale Grammar School, and Seamus Heaney (born 1939; see opposite), who began at Queen's University in 1957.

Heaney graduated from Queen's in 1961 and trained as a teacher at St Joseph's College, where he later taught. He then returned to his old university as a lecturer in 1966 and stayed there until 1972 when he left for County Wicklow. It was while teaching in Belfast that Heaney met Philip Hobsbaum (1932–2005), the poet and critic, who encouraged him and other young poets, including Derek Mahon (born 1941) and Michael Longley (born 1939). In 1965, Heaney's first collection of poems was published in a pamphlet called *Eleven Poems*. His first collection in book form, *Death of a Naturalist*, was published in 1966 and won several important literary prizes. It was the start of an illustrious career in which one of the highest points was receiving the Nobel Prize for Literature in 1995.

ⓘ information

Contact details

Belfast

☎ Tourist Information:
+44 (0)28 9024 6609

🌐 Tourist Information:
www.gotobelfast.com/

Transport links

🚆 Belfast Central

🚗 The M1, the M5 and the A2 run through Belfast

THE BRONTË HOMELAND

COUNTY DOWN

See map p.175 (4)

KEY FIGURES: Patrick, Branwell, Charlotte, Emily and Anne Brontë
KEY LOCATIONS: Emdale; Drumballyroney

This is the part of Ireland where Patrick Brontë (1777–1861), the father of Branwell, Charlotte, Emily and Anne, was born and grew up with his parents, before leaving to study theology at Cambridge University.

Patrick was born into a farming family in the village of Emdale on St Patrick's Day 1777, hence his name, but he had no desire to enter the family trade. Instead, Patrick took every opportunity to learn and, helped by the local rector, managed to win a prized place at Cambridge. Patrick returned to Ireland in 1806 and preached his first sermon at the church in nearby Drumballyroney, but he had not come back to stay.

In 1810, he departed for Yorkshire, where he later married Maria Branwell and became perpetual curate of Haworth in 1820. They had six children, two of whom died in childhood. The others achieved almost iconic status as the

▲ *Patrick Brontë was born and raised in what is now called the Brontë Homeland, near Drumballyroney.*

literary products of a difficult home life. Charlotte was the only one who married; she chose her father's Irish curate, the Reverend Arthur Bell Nicholls, who was brought up in Banagher, Offaly, and who eventually returned there after Charlotte's death in 1855.

(i) information

Contact details

The Brontë Homeland
near Rathfriland
Newry
County Down
BT34

📶 Tourist Information:
www.discovernorthernireland.
com/Bronte-Homeland-
Interpretive-Centre-Rathfriland-
Newry-P2857

Transport links

🚆 Lurgan (14 miles)

🚗 The A1 and A2 run
through Newry

INNISKEEN
COUNTY MONAGHAN

See map p. 175 **5**

KEY FIGURE: Patrick Kavanagh
KEY LOCATION: Patrick Kavanagh Centre

Claimed by many to be Ireland's greatest poet after W. B. Yeats, Patrick Kavanagh (1904–67) was born in Inniskeen. Signposts indicate the house where he lived, although it is privately owned and not open to the public. However, the Patrick Kavanagh Centre, formerly St Mary's Roman Catholic church, which Kavanagh attended and wrote about in *Tarry Flynn* (1948), is full of information about the man and his work.

Kavanagh spent his early years as a farmer, but he yearned to write and left his hometown to become a journalist in Dublin in 1931. He wrote from the heart about what he knew, so his poetry concerns the landscape of County Monaghan and the lives of its inhabitants. He was particularly interested in the contrast between the popular view of 'Oirish' life and its realities. Kavanagh's first collection of poetry, *Ploughman and Other Poems*, was published in 1936 and attracted the

attention of John Betjeman, although his poetry did not really take off until the 1940s.

Kavanagh is probably best known for his epic poem, *The Great Hunger* (1942), which linked the bleak countryside of some parts of Ireland with the sexual repression that he felt made people emotionally barren. There was such outrage when the poem was published that Kavanagh was even questioned by the police about its supposed obscenity. His other works of both prose and poetry included *The Green Fool* (1938), *Collected Poems* (1964) and *Self Portrait* (1964).

In the 1950s and 1960s, Kavanagh lived in Dublin. He died in the city in November 1967 but was buried in Inniskeen. His friends followed his wishes and erected a simple memorial seat to him next to the Grand Canal at Baggot Street Bridge in Dublin. There is a life-size bronze statue of him sitting on a bench on the other side of the canal.

(i) information

Contact details

Inniskeen
Co. Monaghan

☎ +353 (0)42 937 8560

🖥 Patrick Kavanagh Centre: www.patrickkavanagh country.com

Transport links

🚆 Dundalk

🚗 The N53, R178 and R179 run nearby

W. B. YEATS'S IRELAND

GALWAY, SOUTH DUBLIN, SLIGO

See map p.175 **6**

KEY FIGURE: W.B. Yeats; Lady Gregory
KEY LOCATIONS: Coole Park; Rathfarnham; Drumcliff Churychard

W.B. Yeats is one of the most celebrated British poets of all time and in 1923 he became the first Irish poet to win the Nobel Prize for Literature. Yeats took inspiration from many places in Ireland to write his famous poems.

Coole Park

A few walls, a stableyard and a copper beech known as the 'autograph tree' – because it was signed by many famous people – are all that remain of Coole Park. It was once the home of Lady Gregory (1852–1932), the playwright and co-founder of the Abbey Theatre in Dublin. There is, however, a visitor centre to fill in the gaps.

In 1896, Lady Gregory met W.B. Yeats, inviting him to Coole Park the following year. He was recovering from a broken affair with Olivia Shakespear and the visit was a great success. Yeats and Lady Gregory collaborated on books and plays, as well as planning the Irish Literary Theatre, which led on to them setting up the Abbey Theatre in Dublin in 1904.

Lady Gregory was also helpful to Yeats because she gave him the money that enabled him to give up journalism and concentrate on creative writing instead. They continued to have a fruitful and happy friendship until Lady Gregory died at Coole in May 1932. Yeats spent most of the final year of her life staying with her at Coole Park so she was not alone. She was quite infirm by this time, as he noted in his poem 'Coole Park and Ballylee, 1931'.

▼ *Ben Bulben was so treasured by W.B. Yeats that he insisted on being buried near it.*

Rathfarnham

Yeats wanted to find another house that would bring him similar peace to that he enjoyed at Coole Park. In May 1932, he took a lease on Riversdale at Willbrook, just outside Rathfarnham on the south side of Dublin.

It was a barren time for him creatively, caused by a combination of his own ill health and Lady Gregory's death. Yeats had spent much of his life experimenting with psychic matters on the astral plane, and once wrote 'The mystical life is the centre of all that I do and all that I think and all that I write.' So he experienced intellectual curiosity more than anything else when he began to see apparitions at Rathfarnham. A couple of years after Yeats moved in, he saw a child's hand holding a playing card that was either the five of hearts or of diamonds, and wondered whether it meant he had five months or five years to live. As it turned out, it was five years.

Although Yeats's life was coming to a close he was still busy writing, and in 1936 he worked on a translation of the *Upanishads* (1937) and revisions of *A Vision* (1937) at Riversdale. Despite Yeats's ill health, he spent a lot of time travelling to France or visiting friends in England.

▲ *Yeats and his wife Georgiana Hyde-Lees enjoyed automatic writing together, where the stream of thought comes from the unconscious mind.*

Drumcliff Churchyard

The simple headstone on Yeats's grave at Drumcliff bears, at his request, the final lines from his poem, 'Under Ben Bulben'. Ben Bulben was Yeats's adored mountain, which overlooks Drumcliff, where his grandfather was rector.

Yeats died in January 1939 at Roquebrune in France, where his body was temporarily buried. The Dean of St Patrick's Cathedral in Dublin suggested that he should be buried there, but his family obeyed Yeats's wishes and buried him at Drumcliff. However, the start of the Second World War meant that he was not buried until 1948.

(i) information

Contact details

Coole Park Nature Reserve
Gort, Co. Galway

www.coolepark.ie

 Rathfarnham
Ballyboden, Co. South Dublin

www.dublintourist.com/towns/
rathfarnham

Drumcliffe Churchyard
Drumcliffe, Co. Sligo

www.drumcliffe.elphin.anglican
.org

SYNGE'S COTTAGE

ARAN ISLANDS

See map p.175 (7)

KEY FIGURES:	W.B. Yeats; J.M. Synge
KEY LOCATIONS:	Inishmaan; Gregory's Sound; Synge's Chair

W.B. Yeats and J.M. Synge (1871–1909) first met each other in Paris in December 1896. Yeats had already established a reputation for himself as a noted poet, playwright and collector of Irish legends, and he had recently visited the Aran Islands, off Galway Bay, on a fishing trip. Synge, on the other hand, had recently given up his musical training in the hope of becoming a professional writer. Yeats, as the author of *Fairy and Folk Tales of the Irish Peasantry* (1888) and *The Celtic Twilight* (1893), suggested that Synge should visit the Aran Islands to see if inspiration would strike.

Synge made several visits to Inishmaan (the middle of the three Aran Islands) between 1898 and 1902, staying for weeks at a time in the summer or autumn. On each occasion he stayed in a whitewashed cottage near Dún Conchúir that was owned by the MacDonagh family. The cottage has now been turned into a small museum. He enjoyed sitting on the cliffs overlooking Gregory's Sound, tucked into a small, dry-stone shelter that he built himself and which is now known as Synge's Chair.

The visits paid off because Synge wrote a play, *Riders to the Sea* (1904), which was set in Inishmaan and was performed at the Abbey Theatre in Dublin, where Synge became a director in 1906. He followed this with a non-fiction book about Irish peasant life entitled *The Aran Islands* (1907). Synge was also writing other plays, but he was ill and died from Hodgkin's disease in March 1909. Yeats and his patron-collaborator, Lady Gregory, were left with the task of sorting through Synge's manuscripts. Yeats later wrote about some of the ideas that were triggered by Synge's death in *The Death of Synge and Other Passages from an Old Diary* (1928).

(i) information

Contact details

Synge's Cottage, Dûn Chonchúir
Inishmaan, Aran Islands
Co. Galway

+353 (0)99 73 036

Tourist Information:
www.discoverireland.com

Transport links

Inishmaan

HOWTH
COUNTY DUBLIN

See map p.175 (8)

KEY FIGURES: Erskine Childers; W.B. Yeats
KEY LOCATIONS: Howth; Balscadden Cottage; Island Cottage

The strange tale of Erskine Childers has as much excitement as *The Riddle of the Sands* (1903; shown right), the novel for which Childers is most famous. The book is the story of two amateur yachtsmen, Davies and Carruthers, who become amateur spies when they discover German plans for the invasion of England.

Born in Dublin, Childers had great maritime knowledge, which he put to such good use in *The Riddle of the Sands*. In 1914 he became a gun-runner for the Irish Volunteers. First he bought 1,500 second-hand Mauser rifles in Hamburg while everyone thought he was in Mexico, and then he sailed out to the Goodwin Sands in the North Sea in his boat, *Asgard*, to meet the tug bringing the rifles from Germany. He took them on board and brought them ashore at Howth.

Childers fought for the British in the First World War but supported the Irish Republican Army in 1921 and was court-martialed for illegal firearms possession. He was executed by firing squad in November 1922. With characteristic courage, Childers refused a blindfold and shook hands with each member of the firing squad.

Howth was also home to the Yeats family, who moved there from London in the hope of reducing their expenses. 'Willie', as W.B. Yeats was known to his family, was 15 at the time. The family was lent Balscadden Cottage and later moved to Island Cottage near Howth harbour, but a chronic lack of money led them to move back to Dublin in 1884.

ⓘ information

Contact details
Howth
Co. Fingal

🖥 Tourist Information:
www.howthismagic.com

Transport links
🚆 Howth

🚗 The E1/M50 runs nearby

DUBLIN
GREATER DUBLIN

See map p.175   **9**

KEY FIGURES:	James Joyce; W.B. Yeats; J.M. Synge; Samuel Beckett; Jonathan Swift; Oliver Goldsmith; George Bernard Shaw; Bram Stoker
KEY LOCATIONS:	James Joyce Centre; Rathgar; Abbey Theatre; Trinity College; St Patrick's Cathedral; 33 Synge Street; Newman House; Merrion Square

At one time or another, many of the most famous poets, playwrights and novelists have walked the beautiful streets of Dublin. The city's creative hubs are the Abbey Theatre and Trinity College but lots of other places are humming with their own literary legacy.

Joyce's city

Although James Joyce spent most of his life in Europe (including Rome and Zurich), he is indelibly linked with his home city of Dublin.

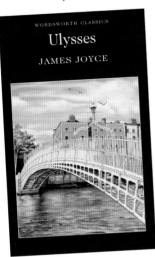

How could he not be when his most famous novel, *Ulysses* (1922, Paris; 1936, England; shown left), describes a single day, 16 June 1904, in the life of the city? Joyce chose this day because it was the date on which he and Nora Barnacle, who later became his wife, walked around the city together shortly after first meeting. It is now annually celebrated as 'Bloomsday' after Leonard Bloom, one of the book's main characters. There are special tours of Dublin that identify the places that appear in the book, such as the Martello tower at Sandycove and 7 Eccles Street, Dublin, which is where Leonard Bloom lived and is marked by a plaque. The original front door of this house is now contained in the James Joyce Centre.

Joyce was born at 41 Brighton Square West, in the Rathgar district of Dublin, in 1882. Joyce wrote from a young age and was influenced by W.B. Yeats and the Norwegian playwright Henrik Ibsen (1828–1906). He moved to Paris in June 1904 with Nora Barnacle and never lived in Ireland again. He died in Zurich in January 1941 and was buried in Fluntern Cemetery there.

Finnegans Wake was published in 1939 and, just like *Ulysses*, served to revolutionize the structure of the novel. Both novels still provoke controversy and much debate.

Abbey Theatre and Yeats

The first Abbey Theatre opened in December 1904 and was founded by W.B. Yeats and Lady Gregory, the playwright and director. It burnt down in a fire in 1951 and a replacement theatre was opened in July 1966.

The original Abbey Theatre was paid for by Annie Horniman (1860–1937), who had been a member of the mystical Order of the Golden Dawn at the same time as Yeats. She enjoyed being his benefactress and supported his desire to create a permanent theatre for the Fays' National Theatre Company, which had been producing his plays.

The first plays to be performed at the Abbey were Yeats's *On Baile's Strand* and *Cathleen ni Houlihan*, and Lady Gregory's comedy, *Spreading the News*. The company went professional in 1906, with Yeats, Lady Gregory and J.M. Synge as the three directors. In 1907, Synge's play, *The Playboy of the Western World*, was premiered at the Abbey and sparked riots because many believed it insulted the inhabitants of the west of Ireland.

In 1925, the Abbey became the first English-speaking state-subsidized theatre when it was given a grant from the government of Eire, which enabled it to continue its tradition of showcasing the best of the Irish playwrights. Among those whose work has been performed here are Padraic Colum (1881–1972); Lennox Robinson (1886–1958), who became the Abbey's manager in 1910 and its director in 1923; Sean O'Casey, whose play *The Plough and the Stars* caused nationalist riots when it was first performed in 1926; and Brian Friel, whose *The Enemy Within*,

▲ W.B. Yeats helped to found the Abbey Theatre, which champions the work of Irish playwrights.

which is based on the exile of St Columba, was first performed at the Abbey in 1962.

Trinity College

Many writers that are associated with Dublin attended Trinity College. Trinity was only open to Protestants until 1793, before which time Catholic students went to University College.

In 1682, Jonathan Swift became a student of Trinity College where he studied with his old schoolfriend William Congreve (1670–1729), who is best remembered for his plays *Love for Love* (1695) and *The Way of the World* (1700).

Oliver Goldsmith was a student here in the 1740s and later wrote the novel *The Vicar of*

Wakefield (1766) and the play *She Stoops to Conquer* (1773). The novelist Bram Stoker distinguished himself at Trinity in the 1860s by winning the University Athletics Championship.

The theatre world also has Trinity College to thank for educating two of its well-loved playwrights: J.M. Synge attended in 1889, as did Samuel Beckett in 1923.

A very important work associated with Trinity College is the Book of Kells, which is held in the Old Library. This was produced in about AD 800 at the monastery on Iona in Scotland, and consists of the four gospels of the New Testament in Latin. The library also contains the Book of Durrow, which is the earliest known Irish illustrated manuscript, dating from between AD 650–80.

St Patrick's Cathedral

Jonathan Swift was born at 7 Hoey's Court, Dublin, and educated at Kilkenny Grammar School. After studying at Trinity College, Swift worked for the diplomat Sir William Temple (1628–99).

Swift had strong Protestant principles – he was ordained in Dublin in 1694 – but these clashed with his political beliefs. He spent a few years in England, but the storm generated by his politics sent him back to Dublin, where he took up the post of Dean of St Patrick's Cathedral in 1713 and continued to write inflammatory pamphlets.

Swift, who is chiefly known for his satirical novel, *Gulliver's Travels* (1726), died in 1745 and was buried in the nave of St Patrick's Cathedral. There is a bust of him on the wall of the south

aisle. The cathedral also contains various items of Swift memorabilia, including the pulpit from where he used to preach.

33 Synge Street

'I am a typical Irishman: my family came from Yorkshire.' This was George Bernard Shaw's typically dry comment on his ancestry. He was born in Synge Street in July 1856 and spent the first 10 years of his life in this house, which was then 3 Upper Synge Street. It was not a happy childhood, as his father was an alcoholic whose

Vandaleur Lee. When Lee went to London, Mrs Shaw and her daughter, Lucy, followed and in April 1876, Shaw joined them. He did not return to Ireland for another 30 years.

Newman House

This Georgian town house, which actually consists of two buildings, Nos. 85 and 86, used to be the Catholic University of Ireland, which later became University College. It was named after Cardinal John Henry Newman (1801–90), who was the first rector of the university. The institution was founded in 1854 and offered Roman Catholic students the chance to attend a university in Dublin, because they were not allowed to take degrees at Trinity College Dublin (see page 187).

James Joyce was one of the Catholic students who studied at the university, and he started there in 1898. Joyce knew Newman House as he once lectured to the Literary and Historical Society in the Physics Theatre, at the back of No. 85. Joyce also knew No. 86, because he studied at the top floor of the house from 1899 to 1902.

The top floor of No. 86 also contains the bedroom that was occupied by the poet Gerard Manley Hopkins while he was Professor of Classics at the university from 1884 to 1889. Hopkins was a Jesuit priest who was overwhelmed by his own sense of failure as a preacher. His period in Dublin was marked by depression and illness, as many of the 'Dark

wholesale grain business was slowly going broke. His mother was an heiress but she was equally impoverished, and the combination was ruinous. The Shaw family moved to another part of Dublin in 1866, and young George went to the Wesley Connexional School (now Wesley College) on St Stephen's Green, followed by many other Dublin schools. However, Shaw's formal education ended at the age of 15, when he became a junior clerk at an estate agency in Molesworth Street.

Meanwhile Shaw's mother was conducting an affair with her singing teacher George John

▲ *The Samuel Beckett Centre at Trinity College is named after the great writer who studied there.*

Sonnets' that he wrote during this time testify. He died from typhoid in 1889 at the age of 54. He was buried in the Jesuit plot in Glasnevin cemetery in Dublin. The playwright Brendan Behan (1923–64) is also buried in Glasnevin, as is Maud Gonne (1866–1953) who was the muse and unrequited love of W.B. Yeats.

Merrion Square

Since this square, the grandest of all the Georgian squares in Dublin, was built in the 1770s, it has attracted many literary writers who are commemorated on the plaques on the buildings.

Joseph Sheridan Le Fanu (1814–73), who was born in Dominick Street, Dublin, and became one of the great masters of the ghost story, moved to 70 Merrion Square after his wife died in 1858. He became increasingly reclusive while he lived here, during which time he wrote several books, including his most chilling collection of tales, *In A Glass Darkly* (1872).

Bram Stoker frequently visited the Wilde family, who were Le Fanu's neighbours at 1 Merrion Square, because he had been at Trinity College with their son, Oscar. Stoker soon began to write theatrical reviews for the *Dublin Evening Mail*, of which Le Fanu was a part-owner. Some of the rooms at 1 Merrion Square are now open to the public, and there is a statue of Oscar Wilde towards the north-west corner of the square.

The Wildes had long since left by the time that W.B. Yeats's wife, George, bought 82 Merrion Square in 1922. Yeats believed that Wilde's excesses had not done literature any favours, so perhaps it is just as well that his family were no longer here. Yeats, George and their children, Anne and Michael, lived in the square until 1928 when they moved to a flat in Fitzwilliam Square.

ⓘ information

Contact details

Dublin
Greater Dublin

📱 Tourist Information:
www.visitdublin.com

☎ +353 1 605 7700

Transport links

🚆 Connolly
Tara Street

🚗 The E1, N2, N3, N81, N11 and M50 all lead to Dublin

Index

Picture Credits

All photography copyright © Chris Coe, except for the following:

Alamy: pages 5, 15 (Marc Hill), 33 (Detail Heritage), 39 (Pictorial Press), 44 (Mike Jenner), 50 (World Pictures), 122, 173 (Mary Evans Picture Library), 190; Belfast Visitor and Convention Bureau: page 179; © The Trustees of the British Museum: pages 27, 80; Corbis: pages 66 (Adam Woolfitt), 142 (Bettmann); Faber and Faber: page 54; © Frederick Warne & Co., 1904, 2002: page 120 (*The Tale of Benjamin Bunny* by Beatrix Potter); Getty Images: pages 5, 11, 20, 32, 45, 121, 128, 130; Harper Collins: pages 16, 23, 126, 143, 154; Harper Collins Children's Books: pages 92, 178; Istockphoto: pages 34 (Graftissimo), 101 (Geogios Kollidas), 168 (Hulton Archive); Library of Congress: pages 42, 56, 81, 139, 149, 150, 156, 187; Little, Brown Book Group: page 87; LondonStills.com: page 70; Mary Evans Picture Library: pages 165 (John Idris Jones), 152 (Thomas Gillmor Collection); Orion Publishing Group: page 151 (Copyright: Rankin); Pan Macmillan: page 95; Penguin Books Ltd: page 14, 46, 92, 125, 185; Puffin Books: page 51, 131; Rex Features: pages 82 (Courtesy Everett Collection), 133 (Nils Jorgensen), 164 (© Warner Bros/Everett); Scholastic Children's Books: page 107; Tony Shaw: page 85; Shutterstock: pages 25 (Paul Cummings), 26–27 (1000 Words), 55 (gumbao), 83 (Tom Curtis), 148 (JeniFoto), 188–189 (sjeacle); David Tipling: page 161; Rob Ware: page 158; Virginia Woolf Society of Great Britain: page 43; West Yorkshire District Council: page 19 (Mark Simons); Wordsworth Editions: pages 12, 186